EUROPEAN UNION (WITHDRAWAL AGREEMENT) ACT 2020

EXPLANATORY NOTES

What these notes do

These Explanatory Notes relate to the European Union (Withdrawal Agreement) Act 2020 (c. 1) which received Royal Assent on 23 January 2020.

- These Explanatory Notes have been prepared by the Department for Exiting the European Union in order to assist the reader of the Act and help inform debate on it. They do not form part of the Act and have not been endorsed by Parliament.

- These Explanatory Notes explain what each part of the Act will mean in practice, provide background information on the development of policy and provide additional information on how the Act will affect existing legislation in this area.

- These Explanatory Notes might best be read alongside the Act. They are not, and are not intended to be, a comprehensive description of the Act.

Table of Contents

These Explanatory Notes relate to the European Union (Withdrawal Agreement) Act 2020 (c.1) which received Royal Assent on 23 January 2020

Commencement 84

Equalities 84

Related documents 85

Annex A – Territorial extent and application in the United Kingdom 86

Annex B – Hansard References 87

Annex C – Glossary 88

These Explanatory Notes relate to the European Union (Withdrawal Agreement) Act 2020 (c.1) which received Royal Assent on 23 January 2020

2

Overview of the Act

1   The European Union (Withdrawal Agreement) Act implements the Withdrawal Agreement, as agreed between the United Kingdom and the European Union (EU). The Act is required to implement the Withdrawal Agreement for it to have domestic legal effect and to enable the UK Government to ratify the Withdrawal Agreement. This Act is also the vehicle for the Government to give effect to the EEA EFTA Separation Agreement between the UK and Norway, Iceland and Liechtenstein, and the Swiss Citizens' Rights Agreement between the UK and Switzerland.

2   The Act provides for the direct application of the Withdrawal Agreement provisions in domestic law where relevant, whilst also recognising the sovereignty of the Parliament of the United Kingdom. The Act amends the EU (Withdrawal) Act 2018 to ensure it reflects the terms of the Withdrawal Agreement. The Act also creates powers to make secondary legislation, where appropriate, to enable the Withdrawal Agreement to be implemented domestically. It includes amendments to the Northern Ireland Act 1998 in relation to rights, safeguards and equality of opportunity protections contained in the Belfast (Good Friday) Agreement 1998. All these measures provide for the implementation of the Withdrawal Agreement agreed between the UK and the EU pertaining to the UK's withdrawal from the EU.

3   This Act also includes provision relating to facilitating access for Northern Ireland goods to the market in Great Britain, as well as further provision to ensure no alteration to the arrangements for North-South co-operation can occur as a result of this Act.

Policy background

4   On 23 June 2016, a referendum was held in the UK and Gibraltar on whether the UK should remain a member of the EU. More than 33.5m people, some 72 per cent of registered voters, voted in the referendum and 52 per cent of those who voted, voted to leave the EU.

5   The European Union (Notification of Withdrawal) Act 2017 was passed into law on 16 March 2017. This gave the Prime Minister the power to notify the European Council of the UK's intention to withdraw from the EU under Article 50(2) of the Treaty on the European Union (TEU). This notification was then given on 29 March 2017.

6   On 26 June 2018, the EU (Withdrawal) Act 2018 passed into law. Its purpose is to provide a functioning statute book when the UK leaves the EU.

7   On 13 November 2017, the previous Government announced its intention to bring forward a new Act to implement the Withdrawal Agreement in domestic law. This confirmed that the major policies set out in the Withdrawal Agreement would be given effect in domestic law through new primary legislation, rather than by secondary legislation under the then EU (Withdrawal) Act.

8   On 14 November 2018, the previous Government published a draft of the Withdrawal Agreement (agreed at negotiator level). This Agreement was agreed by European leaders on 25 November 2018 and laid before Parliament on 26 November 2018.

9   The Agreement was subject to votes in the House of Commons as prescribed under section 13 of the EU (Withdrawal) Act 2018 (EUWA) on 15 January 2019 and 12 March 2019, whilst the Withdrawal Agreement alone, without the Political Declaration, was voted on by the House of Commons on 29 March 2019. The Agreement was rejected in all these votes. The Agreement was also subject to take note motions in the House of Lords.

These Explanatory Notes relate to the European Union (Withdrawal Agreement) Act 2020 (c.1) which received Royal Assent on 23 January 2020

3

10   On 22 March 2019, the European Council and the United Kingdom agreed to an extension to the Article 50 period until 22 May 2019, provided the Withdrawal Agreement was approved by the House of Commons before 29 March 2019, or otherwise until 12 April 2019 (European Council Decision (EU) 2019/476, O.J. No. L 80 I, p.1). The definition of 'exit day' in the EU (Withdrawal) Act 2018 was amended by statutory instrument *The European Union (Withdrawal) Act 2018 (Exit Day) (Amendment) Regulations 2019 (S.I. 2019/718)* to reflect this, having been approved by the House of Commons and the House of Lords on 27 March 2019.

11   On 5 April 2019, the then Prime Minister wrote to the President of the European Council seeking a second extension of the Article 50 period. On 11 April 2019, the European Council and the UK agreed an extension to the Article 50 period until 31 October 2019 (European Council Decision (EU) 2019/584, O.J. No. L 101, p.1). This extension could be terminated early if the Withdrawal Agreement was ratified and came into force before this date. Following the conclusion of the European Council, a statutory instrument *The European Union (Withdrawal) Act 2018 (Exit Day) (Amendment) (No. 2) Regulations 2019 (S.I. 2019/859)*, was made under the negative procedure on 11 April amending the definition of 'exit day'[1] in the EU (Withdrawal) Act 2018 to 31 October 2019 at 11.00 p.m..[2]

12   On 23 May 2019, Prime Minister Theresa May resigned. Following a change in Government, Prime Minister Boris Johnson committed to negotiating a new Withdrawal Agreement. This Withdrawal Agreement was agreed by European leaders at the European Council on 17 October 2019. In addition, the Government made a unilateral declaration concerning the operation of the 'Democratic consent in Northern Ireland' provision of the Protocol on Ireland/Northern Ireland, which was published on the same day.

13   On 19 October 2019, the Government laid before Parliament the new Withdrawal Agreement and new framework for the future relationship between the UK and the EU.

14   On 21 October 2019, the European Union (Withdrawal Agreement) Act was introduced to Parliament. The House of Commons voted for the Act at Second Reading, which passed by 329-299, but the House did not vote in favour of the timetable to debate the Act. Parliament subsequently legislated for an early general election and was dissolved on 6 November 2019.

15   On 19 December 2019, the European Union (Withdrawal Agreement) Bill was introduced to Parliament.

Approach of the European Union (Withdrawal Agreement) Act

16   The UK has a dualist legal system, in which an international treaty ratified by the Government, although binding in international law, does not alter the laws of the state unless and until the treaty is incorporated into domestic law by legislation. This means that the UK Parliament has to pass implementing legislation before an international treaty can have effect domestically.[3] This is a necessary step in the process of ratifying the Withdrawal Agreement as an international treaty.

---

[1] 'Exit day' is defined by the EU (Withdrawal) Act 2018. The date of the UK's departure from the EU is referred to as 'exit day' throughout this document.

[2] Between the first and second extensions of the Article 50 period, the procedure (found at paragraph 14 of Schedule 7 of the EU (Withdrawal) Act 2018) for exercising the power in section 20(4) of the EU (Withdrawal) Act 2018 to change the definition of 'exit day' in that Act was changed from the affirmative to the negative procedure. This was done by section 2 of the EU (Withdrawal) Act 2019, which received Royal Assent on 8 April 2019.

[3] In some cases, it may be that domestic legislation is already sufficient to ensure compliance with the international agreement or that compliance can be delivered without legislation.

These Explanatory Notes relate to the European Union (Withdrawal Agreement) Act 2020 (c.1) which received Royal Assent on 23 January 2020

4

17 The principal purpose of the Act is to implement the Withdrawal Agreement, the separation agreement between the UK and the EEA EFTA countries (EEA EFTA Separation Agreement) and the Swiss Citizens' Rights Agreement (together, 'the Agreements'). Where provisions of the Withdrawal Agreement (or EU law made applicable by it) are capable of having direct effect, the Act enables legal or natural persons to rely directly on those provisions in UK courts. The Act provides for these three Agreements to have an equivalent legal effect in domestic law.

18 The Act is designed to work in conjunction with the EU (Withdrawal) Act 2018. Provisions relating to citizens' rights and the financial settlement will remain separate to that Act, but the implementation of other parts of the Withdrawal Agreement and the additional commitments will require amendments to the Act. Specifically, the Act will amend the EU (Withdrawal) Act 2018 in order to give effect to the implementation period following the repeal of the European Communities Act 1972 (ECA) in section 1 of that Act. This will ensure that sections 2 to 4 of the EU (Withdrawal) Act 2018 will save, and incorporate into domestic law, that EU law which applied in the UK at the end of the implementation period – a date referred to in the Act as 'IP completion day'. This law will then be subject to any changes made by the UK Parliament or the devolved legislatures, consistent with the UK's international obligations. It will also be necessary to amend the EU (Withdrawal) Act 2018 to:

 a. insert the sections directly applying the Agreements (sections 5 and 6) and also to insert the rules of interpretation that will apply to 'relevant separation agreement law' (section 26);

 b. insert the sections which make provision for giving further domestic legislative effect via secondary legislation to provisions of the Agreements that rely explicitly on sections 5 and 6, namely the provisions giving effect to the Other Separation Issues (as defined below) and the Northern Ireland Protocol.

The implementation period

19 The UK and the EU have agreed that the UK's exit will be followed by a time-limited implementation period, which will last until 11.00 p.m. on 31 December 2020 ('IP completion day'). The Act also provides in section 33 that the UK may not agree to an extension of the implementation period in the Joint Committee. During the implementation period, common rules will remain in place, with EU (also known as Union) law continuing to apply to the UK under the terms set out in the Withdrawal Agreement.

20 Therefore, new pieces of directly applicable EU law that are introduced during the implementation period will continue to apply automatically within the UK, in line with Part 4 of the Withdrawal Agreement. Other new EU measures introduced will need to continue to be implemented domestically to comply with Part 4 of the Withdrawal Agreement.

Relationship to EU law

21 On 'exit day', the EU (Withdrawal) Act 2018 will repeal the ECA. Under the terms of Part 4 of the Withdrawal Agreement, it will be necessary to ensure that the EU Treaties and other EU law continues to apply in the UK during the implementation period. This will be achieved by way of transitional provision, by which the Act amends the EU (Withdrawal) Act 2018 so that the effect of the ECA (modified as described below) is saved for the time-limited implementation period.

These Explanatory Notes relate to the European Union (Withdrawal Agreement) Act 2020 (c.1) which received Royal Assent on 23 January 2020

5

22   The Act also modifies the saved ECA provisions to reflect the fact that the UK has left the EU, and that the UK's relationship with EU law during this period is determined by the UK's obligations under the Withdrawal Agreement, rather than as a Member State. The Act will also make sure that existing legislation continues to operate properly during the implementation period, despite the fact that the UK is no longer a Member State. As such, the Act will provide glosses to make clear how EU terms on the UK statute book should be read during the implementation period. For instance, the devolution statutes limit the devolved institutions' competence by reference to EU law. The definition of EU law is, for these purposes, tied to the ECA: it means the rights, obligations etc arising under 'the Treaties' as defined in the ECA. The Act preserves the effect of the ECA for the purposes of the implementation period, and modifies the definition of 'the Treaties' and 'the EU Treaties' to include Part 4 of the Withdrawal Agreement. Therefore, during the implementation period, the references to 'EU law' in the devolution statutes will be read in light of Part 4 of the Withdrawal Agreement and those references will continue to impose restrictions on the competence of the devolved administrations and legislatures, as they did during the period of the UK's membership of the EU.

Interaction with the EU (Withdrawal) Act 2018 and secondary legislation

23   EU rules and regulations will continue to apply in the UK during the implementation period. The Act, therefore, amends the EU (Withdrawal) Act 2018 so that the conversion of EU law into 'retained EU law' and the domestication of historic Court of Justice of the European Union (CJEU) case law can take place at the end of the implementation period rather than on 'exit day'. The Act defines this point in time as 'IP completion day' at section 39.

24   It also includes a power to allow Ministers, following consultation with the judiciary, to change how the EU (Withdrawal) Act 2018 provides for courts to interpret saved historic CJEU case law after the implementation period. Regulations may enable named members of the judiciary to determine the test (and the relevant considerations to apply to it) in deciding whether to depart from any retained EU law.

25   The Act also amends the deficiency-correcting powers in the EU (Withdrawal) Act 2018 to allow them to correct deficiencies arising both from the UK leaving the EU and ceasing to be a Member State and from the termination or any other effect of the implementation period or the Withdrawal Agreement. For instance, deficiencies could arise where:

a.   the law does not function appropriately or sensibly because of the UK's exit from the EU and the end of the implementation period, such as where a piece of legislation references an obligation 'under EU law', which no longer applies at the end of the implementation period. This reference may need to be amended, for instance, to a reference to the obligation under retained EU law, in order for the piece of legislation to continue to function usefully.

b.   reciprocal arrangements which, as a result of Part 4 of the Withdrawal Agreement, no longer apply to the UK at the end of the implementation period. For instance, during the implementation period, the UK will need to continue to report to the European Commission on many issues. On 'IP completion day', the reference to the European Commission could be removed or replaced with reference to a domestic UK body or replacement UK domestic regime.

26   The amendments will not affect the procedures for the scrutiny of secondary legislation made under the EU (Withdrawal) Act 2018, including the system set out in paragraph 3 of Schedule 7 to that Act requiring the 'sifting' of certain statutory instruments proposed to be made by the 'negative' procedure.

These Explanatory Notes relate to the European Union (Withdrawal Agreement) Act 2020 (c.1) which received Royal Assent on 23 January 2020

6

<u>**Governance, enforcement and safeguards**</u>

27   Direct jurisdiction of the CJEU in the UK will come to an end with the implementation period. During the implementation period, the UK and the EU have agreed that the existing EU mechanisms for supervision and enforcement will continue to apply in the UK. This will ensure that EU rules are interpreted and applied consistently in both the UK and the EU for the duration of the implementation period.

28   During the implementation period, the UK will maintain the same recourse to the EU's judicial review structures as a Member State. Should the UK have concerns about the implementation or application of EU law during the implementation period, it will retain the same formal ability to challenge such action as Member States.

29   The ECA currently gives effect to the supremacy of CJEU rulings. This will be preserved during the implementation period, through the saving of the ECA. The Act amends the EU (Withdrawal) Act 2018 so that provisions of that Act which end the jurisdiction of the CJEU in the UK will take effect at the end of the implementation period.

Remaining implementation of the Withdrawal Agreement

30   Article 4 requires that the provisions of the Withdrawal Agreement and the provisions of Union law made applicable by the Withdrawal Agreement produce 'the same legal effects' in the UK as those which they produce within the EU and its Member States. In broad terms (and subject to the provisions of Article 4 itself), the intention is that the Withdrawal Agreement and the provisions of EU law applied by the Withdrawal Agreement have the same legal effects in UK domestic law as attached to EU law while a Member State. One effect of this is that legal or natural persons will be able to rely directly on some of the provisions of the Withdrawal Agreement before the UK courts.

31   The approach in the Act is intended to give effect to Withdrawal Agreement law in a similar way to the manner in which EU Treaties and secondary legislation were given effect through section 2 of the ECA. Although the ECA gives effect to EU Treaties and secondary legislation, it is not the originating source of that law but merely the 'conduit pipe' by which it is introduced into UK domestic law. Further, section 2 of the ECA can only apply to those rights and remedies etc that are capable of being 'given legal effect or used' or 'enjoyed'.[4]

32   The approach in the Act to give effect to Article 4 is to mimic this 'conduit pipe' so that the provisions of the Withdrawal Agreement will flow into domestic law through this Act, in accordance with the UK's obligations under Article 4. The approach also provides for the disapplication of inconsistent or incompatible domestic legislation where it conflicts with the Withdrawal Agreement. This ensures that all rights and remedies etc arising under the Withdrawal Agreement are available in domestic law. The approach in the Act is explained in more detail in the commentary below.

---

[4] R (on the application of Miller and another) (Respondents) v Secretary of State for Exiting the European Union (Appellant) [2017] UKSC 5, paragraph 65. For further explanation of how EU Law applies in the UK please see http://www.legislation.gov.uk/ukpga/2018/16/notes/division/10/index.htm

These Explanatory Notes relate to the European Union (Withdrawal Agreement) Act 2020 (c.1) which received Royal Assent on 23 January 2020

7

33 In some circumstances, provisions contained in the Withdrawal Agreement require further detail to be set out in domestic legislation to ensure rights and obligations etc are given full effect in the UK legal system. For example, Article 159 of the Withdrawal Agreement creates an obligation to establish an independent authority to monitor the implementation and application of the citizens' rights part of the Agreement in the UK. Domestic legislation will be required to establish the authority and to define its powers and purpose in line with the Withdrawal Agreement.

34 In a further example, although a qualifying EU citizen can rely directly in UK courts on some of the provisions of the citizens' rights part of the Withdrawal Agreement, further provision is required to ensure UK legislation gives full effect to and is compatible with those rights. The Act makes provision for how these parts of the Withdrawal Agreement will be implemented.

EEA EFTA Separation Agreement and Swiss Citizens' Rights Agreement

35 In addition to implementing the Withdrawal Agreement, the Act also implements the EEA EFTA Separation Agreement and the Swiss Citizens' Rights Agreement. The UK's obligations under these Agreements are substantively similar to those in the corresponding sections of the Withdrawal Agreement. The EU Settlement Scheme applies to EEA EFTA and Swiss nationals (and their family members) on the same basis as EU citizens through Appendix EU of the Immigration Rules.

36 The Act provides that these two Agreements have an equivalent legal effect in domestic law to that of the Withdrawal Agreement. This will ensure that nationals of Norway, Iceland, Liechtenstein and Switzerland may rely on their rights in the same way as EU citizens. There are limited provisions in the Act specific to the implementation of the EEA EFTA Separation Agreement and the Swiss Citizens' Rights Agreement. Where it is required, further detail is provided in the section by section summary of these notes.

Citizens' rights

37 The Act gives effect to the Withdrawal Agreement so that it applies directly in the UK, underpinning the rights contained within Part 2 of the Withdrawal Agreement in domestic law and providing a means of redress where these rights are not properly implemented, or where other legislation is inconsistent with the Withdrawal Agreement. It will also make provision for the corresponding EEA EFTA Separation Agreement and Swiss Citizens' Rights Agreement. In addition, the Act establishes an independent body to monitor the implementation and application of the citizens' rights part of the Withdrawal Agreement and the EEA EFTA Separation Agreement in the UK.

38 Certain parts of the citizens' rights agreements require additional implementation to operate as intended. To implement these obligations, the Act provides Ministers of the Crown with powers to make provision through secondary legislation. The Act makes further provision for citizens' rights by legislating for:

    a.   rights in relation to entry and residence, including:

          i.   deadlines for applications and temporary protection;

         ii.   rights of frontier workers;

       iii.   restrictions on rights of entry and residence, and retention of existing grounds for deportation; and

       iv.   appeals.

These Explanatory Notes relate to the European Union (Withdrawal Agreement) Act 2020 (c.1) which received Royal Assent on 23 January 2020

8

b.   recognition of professional qualifications;

c.   co-ordination of social security systems;

d.   non-discrimination and equal treatment; and

e.   monitoring of citizens' rights through the establishment of an independent monitoring authority (the IMA).

39   The powers outlined in the paragraphs on the recognition of professional qualifications, social security co-ordination and equal treatment are also available to the devolved administrations, subject to the detailed provisions set out in the commentary below (see paragraphs 174 to 210). The Government can use these powers in areas of devolved competence, but will not normally do so without the agreement of the devolved administrations.

40   In addition to the Act, the Immigration Rules (made under the Immigration Act 1971) deliver the EU Settlement Scheme. The Act makes reference to 'Residence Scheme Immigration Rules' which provide for all EU citizens, EEA EFTA and Swiss nationals, and their family members, resident in the UK to be eligible to apply for leave under the EU Settlement Scheme. This includes citizens who are not meeting the requirements of the Free Movement Directive at the end of the implementation period, or who currently derive an EU right of residence by virtue of their relationship to a UK national, and therefore fall outside the technical scope of the Agreements. All those within scope of the Agreements, or within scope of the UK's domestic implementation of the Agreements, are referred to below as the 'protected cohort'.

Other separation issues

41   The Act provides for the application of EU law in the UK to be brought to an orderly conclusion at the end of the implementation period, particularly in respect of ongoing processes and arrangements. The provisions on the Other Separation Issues provide the technical basis for the winding down of those arrangements to ensure an orderly withdrawal and provide legal certainty for individuals and businesses. For example, the arrangements mean that goods that are placed on the UK or EU market under EU law before the end of the implementation period may continue to circulate freely between the UK and the EU until they reach their end users.

42   The future economic and security relationship between the UK and the EU could supersede the separation provisions agreed in many cases. This may then require new substantive arrangements to be agreed and put in place between the UK and the EU to ensure a smooth and orderly transition from the implementation period to the future relationship. The arrangements set out in the Other Separation Issues are without prejudice to negotiations on the UK's future relationship with the EU.

43   The Other Separation Issues all relate to areas currently governed by EU law. They cover:

a.   goods placed on the market;

b.   ongoing customs procedures;

c.   ongoing VAT and Excise Duty matters;

d.   intellectual property;

e.   ongoing police and judicial co-operation in criminal matters;

f.   ongoing judicial co-operation in civil and commercial matters;

g.   data and information processed or obtained before the end of the implementation period or on the basis of the Withdrawal Agreement;

These Explanatory Notes relate to the European Union (Withdrawal Agreement) Act 2020 (c.1) which received Royal Assent on 23 January 2020

9

h. ongoing public procurement and similar procedures;

i. Euratom related issues;

j. Union judicial and administrative procedures;

k. administrative co-operation procedures;

l. privileges and immunities; and

m. other issues relating to the functioning of the institutions, bodies, offices and agencies of the Union.

44 Where relevant, similar agreement on these matters has also been agreed with the EEA EFTA states as part of the EEA EFTA Separation Agreement.

45 As already set out, the rights and obligations arising under the Agreements will be recognised and available in domestic law by virtue of sections 5 and 6 of the Act. This includes those rights and obligations contained within the Other Separation Issues. In addition to this general implementation, there will be a need to set out some further detail in domestic legislation to ensure that the Other Separation Issues are given full effect in the domestic legal system. For example, on public procurement, EU procurement rules are currently implemented in domestic regulations. These will need some technical amendments to ensure that they continue to function for procurement procedures that are ongoing at the end of the implementation period.

46 The Act will, therefore, include provisions to enable the Government to implement the arrangements on the Other Separation Issues, as set out in Part 3 of the Withdrawal Agreement and the EEA EFTA Separation Agreement. This will be done via a power, exercisable by a Minister of the Crown, which is primarily to be used to adapt existing implementing legislation and regulations made under the EU (Withdrawal) Act 2018. The Government can use this power in areas of devolved competence, but will not normally do so without the agreement of the devolved administrations. An equivalent power will also be available to the devolved administrations, subject to the detailed provisions set out in the commentary below.

Main financial provision

47 The UK and the EU have agreed a financial settlement that covers the payments the UK has committed to making to the EU, and the payments that the UK will receive from the EU. The financial settlement does not address any other costs arising as a consequence of the UK exiting the EU, such as the costs of new administrative arrangements that may need to be put in place by either the UK or the EU, or in relation to the future relationship between the UK and the EU.

48 The methodology for the financial settlement is described in the Joint Report from the Negotiators of the European Union and the United Kingdom Government that was published in December 2017. The Joint Report states that the implementation of the agreed methodology will be based on the following principles:

a. The first principle is that the UK will not finance any commitments that do not require funding from Member States, and will receive a share of any financial benefits that it would have received had it remained a Member State.

These Explanatory Notes relate to the European Union (Withdrawal Agreement) Act 2020 (c.1) which received Royal Assent on 23 January 2020

10

b. The second principle establishes the UK's share of the EU's obligations where they are a component of the settlement. For 2020, the current methodology will be used for determining the UK's annual contributions to the EU budget. For payments after 2020, the UK's share will be the average of its share of the EU budget (taking into account the rebate) over 2014-20.

c. The third principle is that the UK will only be required to make payments as they fall due. The UK will not be required to make payments earlier than would have been the case had it remained a Member State, except for a few specific cases where it might be in the interest of both sides to settle these early. This is particularly relevant for pensions, given that the costs will decline steadily over a long-term period.

49 The Withdrawal Agreement sets out the methodology for calculating the payments to, and receipts from, the EU. It does not set out the final sum that will be paid to the EU. The Withdrawal Agreement does not provide for discretion in the calculation of payments after withdrawal, other than the possible early settlement of certain obligations.

50 To allow the UK Government to meet its international commitments set out in the Withdrawal Agreement, the Act contains a legislative mechanism to authorise payment of those financial obligations.

51 The legislative mechanism in the Act that allows for Withdrawal Agreement obligations to be met during the period from exit day until 31 March 2021 is a 'standing service provision'. This means that payments will be made from the UK's Consolidated Fund, or, if the Treasury so decides, from the National Loans Fund. Spending under this finance authority would wind down as obligations naturally expire under the terms of the Withdrawal Agreement. After 31 March 2021, all obligations payable under the Withdrawal Agreement (other than those relating to the traditional own resources of the EU, such as customs duties which UK authorities have collected on behalf of the EU, which will continue to be paid pursuant to the standing service provision) will be met through supply. The Act also provides that receipts from the EU (e.g. the reimbursement to the UK of the paid-in subscribed capital of the European Investment Bank) and received by a Minister of the Crown or a government department are to be paid into the Consolidated Fund, or if the Treasury so decides, the National Loans Fund.

52 The Act allows payments to be made only in order to meet financial commitments that are required by the Withdrawal Agreement. This finance authority cannot be used for payments relating to the future relationship between the UK and the EU.

Northern Ireland

53 The Protocol on Ireland/Northern Ireland in the Withdrawal Agreement provides arrangements that ensure that the UK (including Northern Ireland) does not remain in a customs union with the European Union. The Protocol also makes arrangements seeking to ensure that there are no checks and controls conducted at or near the border between Northern Ireland and Ireland, as well as providing that the arrangements contained in the Protocol are to be subject to democratic consent in Northern Ireland in relation to their operation and continuation.

54 The Act ensures that the rights and obligations arising under the Withdrawal Agreement will be recognised and available in domestic law by virtue of Article 4 of that Agreement and section 5 of this Act. This includes those rights and obligations contained within the Protocol. This effect will need to be supplemented to ensure that all of the relevant elements of the Protocol and its Annexes are given full effect in the UK legal system.

These Explanatory Notes relate to the European Union (Withdrawal Agreement) Act 2020 (c.1) which received Royal Assent on 23 January 2020

11

55 The Act, therefore, includes provision to enable the Government to implement the arrangements necessary to comply with the Protocol to supplement these general overarching provisions. This will be done via a power exercisable by a Minister of the Crown. The Government can use this power in areas of devolved competence, but will not normally do so without the agreement of the relevant devolved administration. The Act also includes a corresponding power for the devolved authorities to take appropriate steps to give effect to the Protocol in areas that fall within their legislative competences.

56 The UK has committed, in Article 2(1) of the Protocol, to ensure that the UK's withdrawal from the EU will not lead to any diminution of rights, safeguards and equality of opportunity in Northern Ireland, as set out in the 'Rights, Safeguards and Equality of Opportunity' chapter of the Belfast (Good Friday) Agreement 1998. This commitment has effect in domestic law by virtue of section 5. Further provision is made in the Act to give full effect to the UK's commitment in Article 2(1), including a number of amendments to the Northern Ireland Act 1998:

   a. inserting a fetter (i.e. restriction) on the legislative competence and the powers of the Northern Ireland Assembly and Northern Ireland Ministers and departments respectively, preventing them from acting in a way which is incompatible with Article 2(1) of the Protocol; and

   b. giving new functions to two statutory institutions established under the Belfast (Good Friday) Agreement 1998 in Northern Ireland - the Northern Ireland Human Rights Commission (NIHRC) and the Equality Commission for Northern Ireland (ECNI) - to ensure that each commission has the appropriate and necessary statutory functions, respecting their independence and distinct mandates, to take on the role of the dedicated mechanism as provided for by Article 2(1) of the Protocol.

57 An amendment is also made to the Northern Ireland Act 1998 in order to confirm the NIHRC's 'own motion' standing powers to bring proceedings under the Human Rights Act 1998.

58 The power referred to above to implement the Protocol may also be exercised by a Minister of the Crown to facilitate the access of Northern Ireland goods to the market in Great Britain, but cannot be exercised in such a way as to make new arrangements for North-South co-operation.

59 Moreover, the Act makes it clear that a Minister of the Crown cannot agree to the making of a recommendation by the Joint Committee under Article 11(2) of the Protocol that would have the effect of:

   a. altering the arrangements for North-South co-operation as set out in the Belfast (Good Friday) Agreement 1998; or

   b. establishing a new implementation body or amending the functions of an existing implementation body (as defined in the relevant sections of the Northern Ireland Act 1998).

Parliamentary oversight

60 The Act will provide for parliamentary scrutiny over any EU legislation made, or which may be made, during the implementation period that, in the opinion of the European Scrutiny Committee, affects the UK's vital national interests. An equivalent provision is made for the House of Lords European Union Select Committee to perform this role in the House of Lords.

These Explanatory Notes relate to the European Union (Withdrawal Agreement) Act 2020 (c.1) which received Royal Assent on 23 January 2020

12

61 The Act also makes provision for the Withdrawal Agreement to be ratified in a timely manner and avoid additional delay that could be caused by unnecessary requirements. The Act will also repeal unnecessary and spent enactments passed in the previous Parliament in relation to the UK's exit from the EU.

62 Additionally, the Act provides that only Government Ministers may act as UK co-chair of the UK-EU Joint Committee established by the Withdrawal Agreement. This means that the UK co-chair of the Joint Committee will be personally accountable to Parliament for their actions in this forum. Further, the Act prohibits the use of written procedure for adopting Joint Committee recommendations and decisions, ensuring that these are always made by the Minister in person. The Act also requires updates to Parliament on any disputes that may arise after the IP between the UK and the EU.

Legal background

63 For the most part, the relevant legal background is explained in the policy background section of these notes. Where further detail is helpful, it is set out below.

EU (Withdrawal) Act 2018

64 The EU (Withdrawal) Act 2018 repeals the ECA, converts EU law as it stands at the moment of exit into domestic law, and preserves laws made in the UK to implement EU obligations. It also creates temporary powers to make secondary legislation to enable corrections to be made to the laws that would otherwise no longer operate appropriately once the UK has left, so that the domestic legal system continues to function correctly outside the EU. The interaction of the EU (Withdrawal) Act 2018 with the Act is explained in more detail in the relevant sections of these notes.

Citizens' rights

65 Rights in relation to entry and residence:

    a. Free movement rights for EU citizens, EEA EFTA nationals, and Swiss nationals are underpinned by the EU Treaties, Directive 2004/38/EC (the Free Movement Directive), and the EU-Swiss Free Movement of Persons Agreement (FMOPA). These are implemented domestically primarily through the Immigration (European Economic Area) Regulations 2016 (the 'EEA Regulations 2016'). The EEA Regulations 2016 are secondary legislation made under the ECA and the Nationality, Immigration, and Asylum Act 2002. The EEA Regulations 2016 provide for various citizens' rights, including residence rights, appeal rights, and rights of frontier workers[5], and set out thresholds for deportation and exclusion of EU citizens, EEA EFTA nationals, and Swiss nationals.

    b. Free movement covers four broad areas: the right to enter the UK; the right to reside; the right to work; and rights to access benefits and services, and to equal treatment. The citizens' rights provisions in the Act, along with the EU Settlement Scheme established under the Immigration Rules, provide for the domestic implementation of the UK's obligations under the Agreements in these four broad areas.

---

[5]Frontier workers are EU citizens, EEA nationals, or Swiss citizens who pursue employment (including self-employment) in the UK but are not resident in the UK.

These Explanatory Notes relate to the European Union (Withdrawal Agreement) Act 2020 (c.1) which received Royal Assent on 23 January 2020

13

c. As free movement ends, the UK will move away from the EU law framework of rights defined in the EU Treaties, the Free Movement Directive, and FMOPA. The EEA Regulations 2016 will be revoked at the end of the implementation period. In place of the EU law framework of residence, a domestic law framework for residence will be established based on the skills people can contribute to the UK.

d. EU citizens, EEA EFTA nationals, and Swiss nationals, and their family members resident in the UK before the end of the implementation period are already able to apply for residence status under the EU Settlement Scheme.

e. EU citizens, EEA EFTA nationals, and Swiss nationals, and their family members who have been continuously resident in the UK for five years are eligible for settled status, which is also referred to as 'indefinite leave to remain' in current UK immigration law. EU citizens, EEA EFTA nationals, and Swiss nationals, and their family members who have been continuously resident in the UK for less than five years are eligible for 'pre-settled status', also referred to in UK immigration law as 'limited leave to remain'. This means that the individual is granted five years limited leave to remain, and is eligible to apply for settled status as soon as they have completed five years continuous residence in the UK.

f. EU citizens, EEA EFTA nationals, and Swiss nationals with either settled status or pre-settled status will continue to be entitled to work, study, and access public services and benefits on the same basis as they do now. These entitlements for EU citizens, EEA EFTA nationals and Swiss nationals will be subject to future domestic policy changes which apply to UK nationals.

g. As set out in the policy summary section of these notes, the EU Settlement Scheme has been legislated for through Immigration Rules under the Immigration Act 1971. In addition, the Act will enable certain parts of the EEA Regulations 2016 to be saved and modified so that they continue to apply for a specified period to persons within the scope of citizens' rights protections as set out in the Withdrawal Agreement and the Act. The interaction between the EEA Regulations 2016 and the citizens' rights provisions in the Act is explained in detail in the commentary on the provisions of the Act below.

66 Professional qualifications:

a. Directive 2005/36/EC (Professional Qualifications Directive), Directive 98/5/EC (Lawyers Establishment Directive), Directive 2006/43/EC (Audit Directive), and Council Directive 74/556/EEC (Professions involving trade, distribution and professional use of toxic products) provide for the recognition of professional qualifications. EU citizens and EEA EFTA nationals and their family members residing or working in the UK at the end of the implementation period with recognitions under these Directives will continue to have qualifications recognised under the Withdrawal Agreement and EEA EFTA Separation Agreement.

b. Swiss nationals with recognised qualifications under Directive 2005/36/EC, Directive 98/5/EC, Council Directive 74/556/EEC, Council Directive 86/653/EEC (concerning self-employed commercial agents) will continue to have qualifications recognised under the Swiss Citizens' Rights Agreement. Certain service providers will also, for a 5 year period after the end of the implementation period, be able to rely on Council Directive 77/249/EEC (to facilitate the effective exercise by lawyers of freedom to provide services) and Title II of Directive 2005/36/EC (temporary and occasional provision of services) to use their qualifications to continue to provide services if certain conditions are met.

These Explanatory Notes relate to the European Union (Withdrawal Agreement) Act 2020 (c.1) which received Royal Assent on 23 January 2020

14

c. In the UK, these directives are implemented via both primary and secondary legislation including the EU (Recognition of Professional Qualifications) Regulations 2015, the European Communities (Recognition of Professional Qualifications) Regulations 2007 and sector specific legislation such as the Medical Act 1983. The European Communities (Lawyer's Practice) Regulations 2000 and the European Communities (Lawyer's Practice) (Scotland) Regulations 2000 implement the Lawyers Establishment Directive. The rights of approved statutory auditors are implemented in domestic law under Part 42 of the Companies Act 2006.

d. During the implementation period, individuals with professional qualifications may continue to apply for recognition of those qualifications. For those in scope of the residence parts of the Withdrawal Agreement and EEA EFTA Separation Agreement, any qualifications recognised, or in the process of recognition, by the end of the implementation period will continue to be recognised. Decisions on recognition of qualifications sought after the end of the implementation period will be subject to the outcome of future relationship negotiations.

e. For those in scope of the Swiss Citizens' Rights Agreement, any qualifications recognised, or in the process of recognition, by the end of the implementation period will continue to be recognised. It has also been agreed that any Swiss or UK national with a qualification, or in the process of obtaining a qualification at the end of the implementation period, can apply for recognition of their qualifications within four years of the end of the implementation period.

67 Co-ordination of social security systems:

a. This part is underpinned by the EU regulations on social security co-ordination, which protect the social security position of persons who move and work around the EU. These are Regulations (EC) 883/2004 and 987/2009, and Regulations (EEC) 1408/71 and 574/72 in respect of third country nationals in the UK.

b. The EU regulations on social security co-ordination will continue to apply in the UK at the end of the implementation period for persons in scope of the Agreements. The Act will ensure that the EU regulations will have the same legal effect in the UK as they do in Member States. Further explanation as to the application of EU social security co-ordination regulations in the UK via the Act is provided in the commentary section below.

68 Equal treatment:

a. Articles 18, 21, 45 and 49 of the Treaty on the Functioning of the EU (TFEU), Article 24 of Directive 2004/38 and Regulation (EU) 492/2011 provide for the prohibition of discrimination on the grounds of nationality and for equal treatment between EU citizens and nationals of the host state. There are similar protections in the EEA EFTA Separation Agreement and the FMOPA.

b. For persons residing and working in the UK on the basis of the Agreements, the prohibition on discrimination on grounds of nationality and rights to equal treatment will continue. Further explanation as to how the Act provides for this is explained below.

These Explanatory Notes relate to the European Union (Withdrawal Agreement) Act 2020 (c.1) which received Royal Assent on 23 January 2020

15

Territorial extent and application

69 Section 42 sets out the territorial extent of the Act; that is the jurisdictions that the provisions in the Act are intended to form part of the law.

70 This Act extends to the whole of the UK. In addition, repeals and amendments made by the Act have the same territorial extent as the legislation that they are repealing or amending. For example, section 1 of the EU (Withdrawal) Act 2018, which repeals the ECA, extends to Gibraltar and the three Crown Dependencies (the Channel Islands and the Isle of Man) to the extent that the ECA itself extended to those territories. This means the saving of the ECA in section 1 (which will alter the effect of section 1 of the 2018 Act), will extend to those jurisdictions to the same extent as the original Act.

71 The power in section 36 of the Immigration Act 1971 or (as the case may be) section 60(4) of the UK Borders Act 2007 may also be exercised to extend to the Isle of Man or any of the Channel Islands the modifications made to that Act by section 10 of the Act.

72 Further, paragraphs 1 and 2 of Schedule 5, which provide for the deferral of subordinate legislation to the end of the implementation period, extend outside the UK to the extent that any subordinate legislation which they modify so extends.

73 Beyond this, as Gibraltar and the Crown Dependencies normally legislate for themselves to give effect to relevant obligations under international agreements - as is the case with Gibraltar under the Constitution of Gibraltar 2006 - the Act does not extend to those territories.

74 The UK Parliament does not normally legislate with regard to matters that are within the legislative competence of the Scottish Parliament, the National Assembly for Wales or the Northern Ireland Assembly without the consent of the legislature concerned. It is also the practice of the Government to seek the consent of the devolved legislatures for provisions which would alter the competence of those legislatures or the devolved administrations in Scotland, Wales and Northern Ireland.

75 The legislative consent is set out at Annex A.

These Explanatory Notes relate to the European Union (Withdrawal Agreement) Act 2020 (c.1) which received Royal Assent on 23 January 2020

16

Commentary on provisions of the Act

Section 1: Saving of ECA for implementation period

76   This section inserts a new section 1A into the EU (Withdrawal) Act 2018. New section 1A saves and amends the ECA for the purpose of giving effect to Part 4 of the Withdrawal Agreement. Until 'exit day', the ECA's purpose is to implement EU law as required by the UK's membership of the EU; during the implementation period, by contrast, the modified and repurposed 1972 Act will implement EU law as set out in the Withdrawal Agreement.

77   Subsection (1) makes clear that the provisions in the following subsections (2) to (4) will have effect despite the repeal of the ECA on 'exit day'.

78   Subsection (2) provides for the ECA to continue to have effect in domestic law, subject to the modifications repurposing that Act so that it works to give effect to the implementation period at subsections (3) to (5). To the extent the ECA currently has any effect in the law of a relevant territory - the Isle of Man, any of the Channel Islands or Gibraltar - it will continue to have the same effect for the purposes of the implementation period.

79   Subsection (3) modifies the saved ECA, so as to ensure that it gives effect to EU law in the UK for the purposes of the implementation period at Part 4 of the Withdrawal Agreement. Specifically:

    a.   (3)(a)(i) adds Part 4 of the Withdrawal Agreement, except those provisions that relate to the Common Foreign and Security Policy, to the definition of 'the Treaties' and 'the EU Treaties' in section 1(2) of the ECA. This means that international agreements concluded by the EU and which enter into force during the implementation period will be given effect to via Part 4 of the Withdrawal Agreement.

    b.   (3)(a)(ii) takes a snapshot of what falls within the definition of 'the Treaties' and 'the EU Treaties' on exit day. Article 129(4) of the Withdrawal Agreement states that 'the United Kingdom may negotiate, sign and ratify international agreements entered into in its own capacity in the areas of exclusive competence of the Union, provided those agreements do not enter into force or apply during the transition period, unless so authorised by the Union'. (3)(a)(ii) also provides a power to Ministers to exclude an international agreement from the definition of Treaties / EU Treaties where appropriate, to cater for the eventuality where the UK negotiates, signs and ratifies an international agreement during the implementation period in an area of EU exclusive competence, the EU authorises the UK to bring it into force or for it to apply during the implementation period, and in order to do so, the UK needs to remove an existing EU-third country international agreement given effect to via the ECA, and which conflicts with this new international agreement, from the definition of 'the Treaties'.

    c.   (3)(b) amends section 2(2) of the ECA so that the reference in that section to the 'objects of the EU' becomes a reference to those objects so far as they are applicable to and in the UK by virtue of Part 4 of the Withdrawal Agreement. This modifies section 2(2) of the ECA so that it functions to give effect to the UK's EU obligations as per Part 4 of the Withdrawal Agreement on the implementation period.

These Explanatory Notes relate to the European Union (Withdrawal Agreement) Act 2020 (c.1) which received Royal Assent on 23 January 2020

d. (3)(c) removes section 2(3) of the ECA. Section 2(3) authorised payments due under the Treaties to be made to the EU. In order to allow for payments due under the Withdrawal Agreement the UK will rely on section 20 of the Act, which provides for payments to be made under a standing service provision until March 2021, after which payment will be made under the system of supply.

e. (3)(d) modifies section 3(1) of the ECA, so that in legal proceedings questions regarding the meaning or effect of the Withdrawal Agreement during the implementation period shall be treated as a question of law. Such questions are to be determined by the domestic court, in accordance with relevant decisions of the CJEU in line with Part 4 of the Withdrawal Agreement.

f. (3)(e) specifically modifies sections 5 and 6 of the ECA (concerning customs duties and the Common Agricultural Policy (CAP)) to make sure that they continue to operate properly during the implementation period and to avoid any suggestion that the Act merely preserves CAP arrangements and customs duties etc as they had effect at the moment of withdrawal.

g. (3)(f) modifies Part 2 of Schedule 1 of the ECA:

   i. (i) modifies the definition of 'EU customs duty' so that any reference to such provision is a reference to it so far as it is applicable to and in the UK by virtue of Part 4 of the Withdrawal Agreement during the implementation period;

   ii. (ii) modifies the definition of 'Member State' that will apply in domestic law during the implementation period.

80 Subsection (4) provides a definition for 'relevant territory' being any territory to which the ECA has applied in any limited capacity previously. Specifically, the term includes the Isle of Man, any of the Channel Islands or Gibraltar.

81 Subsection (5) will repeal subsections (1) to (4) at the end of the implementation period, referred to as 'IP completion day' in the Act. This will be at the point the implementation period ends, i.e. 11.00 p.m. on 31 December 2020.

82 Subsection (6) clarifies the meaning of various terms referenced in this section, specifically:

   a. 'implementation period' - implementation or transition period, as provided for by Part 4 of the Withdrawal Agreement and beginning with 'exit day' and ending on 'IP completion day';

   b. 'IP completion day' - as defined in section 39(1) of the Act, is 31 December 2020 at 11.00 p.m., unless amended by regulations under section 39(4) of the Act to take account of any changes to EU summertime arrangements; and

   c. 'Withdrawal Agreement' - as defined in section 39(1) of the Act, is the agreement between the United Kingdom and the EU under Article 50(2) of the TEU which sets out arrangements for the United Kingdom's withdrawal from the EU.

83 Subsection (7) clarifies that:

   a. references to the ECA are to be read as being or as including references to the repurposed and saved version of that Act so far as the context permits or requires; and

These Explanatory Notes relate to the European Union (Withdrawal Agreement) Act 2020 (c.1) which received Royal Assent on 23 January 2020

18

b. references to any part of the Withdrawal Agreement or of the EEA EFTA Separation Agreement also include references to a different part of that agreement so far as apply to that part. Provisions in other parts of the Withdrawal Agreement will, therefore, be caught by the term 'Part 4 of the Withdrawal Agreement', so far as those provisions apply to Part 4, for example, the definitions in Article 2 of the Withdrawal Agreement.

Section 2: Additional saving for implementation period

84 This section inserts a new section 1B into the EU (Withdrawal) Act 2018. Section 1B saves existing EU-derived domestic legislation and ensures that EU-related references continue to operate properly during the implementation period.

85 Subsection (1) makes clear that subsections (2) to (5) have effect despite the repeal of the ECA on exit day.

86 Subsection (2) makes clear that EU-derived domestic legislation continues to have effect in domestic law on and after exit day, as it had effect in domestic law immediately before exit day. EU-derived domestic legislation is defined in subsection (7). EU-derived domestic legislation is saved to avoid the risk of legislation lapsing, or being impliedly repealed or emptied of meaning, given that the UK will no longer be a Member State of the EU and the ECA will have been repealed by section 1 of the EU (Withdrawal) Act 2018.

87 Specifically, so far as the context permits or requires, subsection:

a. (3)(a) makes it clear that references to the definitions listed in Part 2 of Schedule 1 of the ECA that appear in Schedule 1 of the Interpretation Act 1978 or elsewhere, have effect in EU-derived domestic legislation as they have been modified by sections 1A(2) to (4) of the EU (Withdrawal) Act 2018. For instance, the modified definition of 'Member State' in new section 1A(3)(f)(ii) is reflected in the definitions contained in Schedule 1 to the Interpretation Act 1978. Because the definitions in the 1978 Act apply across the statute book, new section 1B(3)(a) makes clear that references to 'Member State' in EU-derived legislation should pick up on the new modified definition in the ECA.

b. (3)(b)(i) provides for references to cases, general EU law principles and the term 'EU law' itself (among other things) to be read as they apply in the UK by virtue of Part 4 of the Withdrawal Agreement.

c. (3)(b)(ii) ensures that any reference to an EU Treaty or part of an EU Treaty, for instance provisions of the TFEU or the TEU, remain relevant insofar as those provisions continue to apply in the UK by virtue of Part 4 of the Withdrawal Agreement.

d. (3)(b)(iii) provides for references to EU measures in domestic legislation to be references to the EU instrument read in light of Part 4 of the Withdrawal Agreement.

e. (3)(b)(iv) provides that any part of EU law not caught by (3)(a)(ii) and (iii) will also be read in light of Part 4 of the Withdrawal Agreement.

f. (3)(b)(v) provides for references to any tax, duty, levy or interests of the EU to be read as continuing to apply to the UK, where applicable under Part 4 of the Withdrawal Agreement.

g. (3)(b)(vi) provides for any arrangement involving or relating to the EU not covered by existing provisions in (3)(a) should be read as a reference to that arrangement provided that the arrangement is applicable to and in the UK by virtue of Part 4 of the Withdrawal Agreement.

These Explanatory Notes relate to the European Union (Withdrawal Agreement) Act 2020 (c.1) which received Royal Assent on 23 January 2020

19

h. (3)(c) provides that any reference to the ECA, subject to section 1B(3)(a), is to the saved and repurposed ECA as a result of the modifications made at 1A(2) to (4) of this Act.

i. (3)(d) makes sure that any reference to the EU or EEA territory includes the UK.

j. (3)(e) provides for references to citizens of the EU or nationals of the EEA across the UK statute book to include UK nationals, as defined in Article 2 of the Withdrawal Agreement.

k. Finally, (3)(f) provides two further glossing mechanisms:

   i. first, (3)(f)(i) enables further glosses to be added by regulations made under powers located elsewhere in the EU (Withdrawal) Act 2018: in sections 8A and Part 1A of Schedule 2;

   ii. second, (3)(f)(ii) directs a court or any other reader of the law to interpret EU-derived legislation, which is not the subject of a specific gloss but is capable of being ascertained from Part 4 of the Withdrawal Agreement, in line with that Part of the Agreement.

88 Subsection (4) applies the glosses in subsection (3), to any new EU-derived domestic legislation that is made or passed during the implementation period for the purposes of implementing ongoing EU obligations or otherwise relates to the EU or EEA law. It also disapplies these subsections from applying to legislation made during the implementation period which is subject to contrary intent, such as where legislation is made during the implementation period for a purpose to which the glosses should not apply.

89 Subsection (5) makes both the saving of EU-derived domestic legislation and its modification by the glosses subject to regulations made under the Act and under the EU (Withdrawal) Act 2018, specifically regulations made under new section 8A, section 23 or Part 1A of Schedule 2. Regulations will therefore be able to make exceptions to the glosses in particular cases where applying the glosses would not produce the correct result.

90 Subsection (6) repeals subsections (1) to (5) on IP completion day.

91 Subsection (7) defines 'EU-derived domestic legislation'. It essentially mirrors the definition in section 2 of the EU (Withdrawal) Act 2018:

   a. paragraph (a) relates to secondary legislation made under the dedicated power in section 2(2) of the ECA to implement the UK's obligations under EU law, including under paragraph 1A of Schedule 2 ECA (this allows for ambulatory cross-references to 'EU instruments');

   b. paragraph (b) is designed to cover legislation which, while not made under section 2(2) of the ECA, was either specifically passed (e.g. by an Act of Parliament) or made under other secondary legislation making powers for the purpose of implementing EU obligations;

   c. paragraph (c) covers enactments which are connected to, but do not fall within, the definitions of domestic legislation preserved by subsection (7)(a) or (7)(b) or converted EU law. It is designed to ensure that provisions which are tied in some way to EU law, or to domestic law which implements EU law, can continue to operate properly post exit; and

These Explanatory Notes relate to the European Union (Withdrawal Agreement) Act 2020 (c.1) which received Royal Assent on 23 January 2020

20

d.   paragraph (d) is a residual category designed to cover provisions which relate in some other way to the EU or EEA. For example, if an Act of Parliament included a cross- reference to a definition contained in an EU instrument or simply contained references which are EU related, those provisions would fall within the definition and would be EU-derived domestic legislation.

92   The definition of 'EU-derived domestic legislation' excludes any provision of the ECA, the EU (Withdrawal) Act 2018, this Act and any provisions in regulations made under either the 2018 Act or this Act.

93   The glosses set out in this section will impact the devolution statutes for each devolved administration, providing for the current EU law limit on devolved competence to be modified for the duration of the implementation period. The devolution statutes limit the devolved institutions' competence by reference to EU law. The definition of EU law is, for these purposes, tied to the ECA - it means the rights, obligations etc arising under the 'EU Treaties' as defined in the ECA. This Act preserves the effect of the ECA for the purposes of the implementation period, and modifies the definition of 'EU Treaties' to include Part 4 of the Withdrawal Agreement. As a result, the devolved administrations will not be able to act incompatibly with Part 4 of Withdrawal Agreement, and the restrictions of devolved competence are maintained for the duration of the implementation period.

Section 3: Supplementary power in connection with implementation period

94   This section provides Ministers of the Crown with a supplementary power in connection with the implementation period. This power is inserted into the EU (Withdrawal) Act 2018 as new section 8A.

95   New section 8A(1) contains a power for a Minister of the Crown to make the following provision by regulations in connection with the implementation period:

a.   to specify additional glosses for EU-related terms in EU-derived domestic legislation so that the statute book continues to function during the implementation period;

b.   to disapply:

   i.   the glosses in new section 1B(3) which apply to EU-derived domestic legislation saved on exit day, so that EU-related terms can be read without the glosses;

   ii.   the application of the glosses by new section 1B(4) to EU-derived domestic legislation passed or made between exit day and IP completion day, so that EU-related terms in such legislation can be read without the gloss;

c.   to make different provision from new section 1B(3) or (4), so that specific provision can be made for particular EU-related terms, so as to enable the statute book to continue to work effectively during the implementation period. This means a different approach to the general gloss can be taken in order to suit specific circumstances;

d.   to amend or repeal provisions in the EU (Withdrawal) Act 2018 in consequence of the automatic repeals by new sections 1A(5) and 1B(6) of the main provisions in the EU (Withdrawal) Act 2018 that implement the implementation period. Such amendments to the Act might be necessary in the interests of clarity and certainty. The Act will have been substantially amended to provide for the implementation period. At the end of that period, many of these modifications will no longer be applicable and therefore should be removed in order for the law to function clearly; and

These Explanatory Notes relate to the European Union (Withdrawal Agreement) Act 2020 (c.1) which received Royal Assent on 23 January 2020

21

e.   to make provision, not covered by paragraphs (a) to (d) above, but which is appropriate for the purposes of, or otherwise in connection with, Part 4 of the Withdrawal Agreement. For example, there may be legislative references to the UK's membership of or participation in EU bodies that are no longer meaningful during the implementation period and so should be removed.

96   Subsection (2) provides that supplementary provision made under this power might include modifying (such as amending, repealing or revoking) both primary and secondary legislation. The power may not be used to do all the things that an Act of Parliament can do.

97   Subsection (3) clarifies that the supplementary power may not be used to modify primary legislation passed or made after IP completion day (or subordinate legislation made under that primary legislation).

98   Subsection (4) sunsets the power so that no regulations may be made under this section after the end of the period of two years beginning with IP completion day.

Section 4: Powers corresponding to section 3 involving devolved authorities

99   This section inserts a new Part 1A, *Supplementary powers in connection with implementation period,* into Schedule 2 to the EU (Withdrawal) Act 2018. That Schedule confers on devolved authorities certain powers corresponding to powers conferred on a Minister of the Crown by the 2018 Act.

100 New paragraph 11A(1) of Schedule 2 to the EU (Withdrawal) Act contains a power for a devolved authority to make the following provision by regulations in connection with the implementation period:

a.   to specify additional glosses for EU-related terms in EU-derived domestic legislation so that the statute book continues to function during the implementation period;

b.   to disapply:

i.   the glosses in new section 1B(3) which apply to EU-derived domestic legislation saved on exit day, so that EU-related terms can be read without the glosses;

ii. the application of the glosses by new section 1B(4) to EU-derived domestic legislation passed or made between exit day and IP completion day, so that EU-related terms can be read without the gloss;

c.   to make different provision from new section 1B(3) to (4), so that specific provision can be made for particular EU-related terms, so as to enable the statute book to continue to work effectively during the implementation period. This means a different approach to the general gloss can be taken in order to suit specific circumstances;

d.   to make provision, not covered by paragraphs (a) to (c) above, but which is appropriate for the purposes of, or otherwise in connection with, Part 4 of the Withdrawal Agreement. For example, there may be legislative references to the UK's membership of or participation in EU bodies that are no longer meaningful during the implementation period and which should be removed.

101 New paragraph 11A(2) provides that a Minister of the Crown acting jointly with a devolved authority may by regulations make the following provision in connection with the implementation period:

a.   to specify additional glosses for EU-related terms in EU-derived domestic legislation so that the statute book continues to function during the implementation period;

These Explanatory Notes relate to the European Union (Withdrawal Agreement) Act 2020 (c.1) which received Royal Assent on 23 January 2020

22

    b. to disapply:

        i. the glosses in new section 1B(3) which apply to EU-derived domestic legislation saved on exit day, so that EU-related terms can be read without the glosses;

        ii. the application of the glosses by new section 1B(4), so that specific provision can be made for particular EU-related terms, so as to enable the statute book to continue to work effectively during the implementation period. This means a different approach to the general gloss can be taken in order to suit specific circumstances;

    c. to make different provision from new section 1B(3) to (4), so that specific provision can be made for particular EU-related terms, so as to enable the statute book to continue to work effectively during the implementation period. This means a different approach to the general gloss can be taken in order to suit specific circumstances;

    d. to make provision, not covered by paragraphs (a) to (c) above, but which is appropriate for the purposes of, or otherwise in connection with, Part 4 of the Withdrawal Agreement. For example, there may be legislative references to the UK's membership of or participation in EU bodies that are no longer meaningful during the implementation period and which should be removed.

102 New paragraph 11A(3) provides that supplementary provision made under these powers might include modifying (such as amending, repealing or revoking) both primary and secondary legislation. The power may not be used to do all the things that an Act of Parliament can do.

103 New paragraph 11A(4) clarifies that the supplementary power may not be used to modify primary legislation passed or made after IP completion day (or subordinate legislation made under that primary legislation).

104 New paragraph 11A(5) sunsets the power so that no regulations may be made under this section after the end of the period of two years beginning with IP completion day.

105 New paragraph 11A(6) provides that regulations made by the devolved authorities acting alone under the power in paragraph 11A(1) are subject to the provisions of paragraphs 11B and 11C below.

No power to make provision outside devolved competence

106 New paragraph 11B provides that a devolved authority acting alone cannot exercise the power to make supplementary provision for the implementation period unless the provision is within devolved competence, as defined in paragraphs 11D to 11F.

Certain requirements for consent, joint exercise or consultation

107 New paragraph 11C provides that any requirements for consent, joint exercise or consultation with the UK Government will apply where the type of provision made by a devolved authority acting alone under this power would, if made under other powers, require UK Government consent, consultation or joint exercise of powers, as provided for in paragraphs 5 to 7 of Part 1 of Schedule 2 of the EU (Withdrawal) Act 2018.

Meaning of devolved competence: Part 1A

108 Paragraphs 11D, 11E and 11F define devolved competence in relation to the exercise of the power to make supplementary provision in connection with the implementation period.

These Explanatory Notes relate to the European Union (Withdrawal Agreement) Act 2020 (c.1) which received Royal Assent on 23 January 2020

23

Section 5: General implementation of remainder of withdrawal agreement

109 This section gives effect to Article 4 of the Withdrawal Agreement, on the methods and principles relating to the effect, the implementation, and the application of the Withdrawal Agreement.

110 Article 4 of the Withdrawal Agreement provides for:

    a.   individuals and businesses to be able to rely directly on the terms of the Withdrawal Agreement to bring a claim before UK courts, where certain tests are met;

    b.   the disapplication of provisions of domestic law which are inconsistent or incompatible with the Withdrawal Agreement; and

    c.   provisions of the Withdrawal Agreement referring to EU law and its concepts to be interpreted and applied in the UK using the methods and general principles of EU law.

111 Article 4 also states that provisions of the Withdrawal Agreement which are based on EU law must be interpreted in the UK in conformity with CJEU case law handed down before the end of the implementation period, and that the UK's courts need to have due regard to relevant CJEU case law handed down after this point when interpreting and applying relevant areas of the Withdrawal Agreement.

112 In order to give effect to Article 4, this section, which will be inserted into the EU (Withdrawal) Act 2018, makes the rights and obligations etc in the Withdrawal Agreement available in domestic law. This section also provides that domestic legislation must be read, and given effect, in a manner that is compatible with the Withdrawal Agreement.

113 Taken together, subsections (1) and (2) ensure that rights, powers, obligations, remedies etc as they arise or are created from time to time in the Withdrawal Agreement are given legal effect in the UK legal system. This means that they will apply directly without the need for further domestic implementing legislation. This also means that the limited category of dynamic provisions of the Withdrawal Agreement will flow through the 'conduit pipe' of this section into domestic law as they update post-exit.

114 Specifically, subsection (1) provides for rights, powers, liabilities, obligations and restrictions created or arising under the Withdrawal Agreement, and remedies and procedures provided for by the Withdrawal Agreement, to apply directly in domestic law.

115 Subsection (2) makes clear that the rights and obligations etc arising from the Withdrawal Agreement and which will apply directly in the UK by subsection (1) are to be recognised in domestic law and enforced, allowed and followed accordingly.

116 Subsection (3) provides that enactments are to be read and have effect subject to subsection (2). 'Enactment' is defined at section 39 and, for the purposes of the Act, means *an enactment whenever passed or made* and therefore captures legislation (examples of which are given in section 39) even if passed after the Act is passed. Therefore, the effect of this section is to ensure that any past or future enactment which does not clearly state otherwise (including any enactment contained within the Act itself), will take effect subject to section 5(2).

117 Subsection (4) makes clear that this section will not apply in relation to Part 4 of the Withdrawal Agreement (Implementation period) so far as section 2(1) of the ECA applies in relation to that Part.

These Explanatory Notes relate to the European Union (Withdrawal Agreement) Act 2020 (c.1) which received Royal Assent on 23 January 2020

24

118 Subsection (5) directs the reader to look also at the specific parts of the Act which make further provision for giving effect to the Withdrawal Agreement - namely, citizens' rights, financial provision, the interpretation of law relating to the Agreements etc, certain other separation issues, and the corresponding powers for the devolved administrations. This list is not exhaustive, and the reader should look to all pieces of legislation which may be relevant.

Section 6: General implementation of related EEA EFTA and Swiss agreements

119 This section concerns the general implementation of the EEA EFTA Separation Agreement and the Swiss Citizens' Rights Agreement. This section ensures a consistent approach across these Agreements by following the same approach to implementation as that set out in section 5.

120 This is done by broadly replicating the approach taken in Article 4 of the Withdrawal Agreement and applying that to the EEA EFTA Separation Agreement and the Swiss Citizens' Rights Agreement. This is achieved by ensuring that subsections (1) and (2) of section 6 mirror subsections (1) and (2) of section 5.

121 Taken together, subsections (1) and (2) ensure that rights, powers, obligations, remedies etc as they arise or are created from time to time in the EEA EFTA Separation Agreement or the Swiss Citizens' Rights Agreement are given legal effect in the UK. This means that they will apply directly without the need for the UK Parliament to pass further domestic implementing legislation. This also means that the limited category of dynamic provisions of these agreements will flow through the 'conduit pipe' of this section into domestic law as they update post-exit. While there is no express requirement in these Agreements to provide for implementation in this manner, this approach ensures consistency across the Agreements and, subject to any differences between the Agreements, gives rise to consistent rights and remedies for EEA EFTA and Swiss individuals and firms, and EU individuals and firms. Subsection 3 provides that in the unlikely event of any conflict between the terms of either the EEA EFTA Separation Agreement or the Swiss Citizens' Rights Agreement on the one hand, and the Withdrawal Agreement on the other, the terms of the latter shall take precedence.

122 Specifically, subsection (1) provides for rights, powers, liabilities, obligations and restrictions remedies or procedures that would from time to time be created or arise, or be provided for, by or under the EEA EFTA Separation Agreement or the Swiss Citizens' Rights Agreement, and which would, in accordance with Article 4(1) of the Withdrawal Agreement be required to be given legal effect or used in the UK without need for further enactment, to apply in the UK as if Article 4(1) of the Withdrawal Agreement applied to them and those Agreements were part of EU law and the relevant EEA States and Switzerland were Member States.

123 Subsection (2) makes clear that the rights and obligations etc arising from the Agreements, and which will apply directly in the UK by virtue of subsection (1) are to be recognised in domestic law and enforced, allowed and followed accordingly.

124 Subsection (3) provides that enactments are to be read and have effect subject to subsection (2). 'Enactment' is currently defined at section 39 and, for the purposes of the Act, means 'an enactment whenever passed or made' and therefore captures legislation (examples of which are given in section 39) even if passed after the Act. Thus the effect of this section is to ensure that any past or future enactment (except for the new section 7A of the EU (Withdrawal) Act 2018 but otherwise including an enactment contained within that Act) will take effect subject to subsection (2).

These Explanatory Notes relate to the European Union (Withdrawal Agreement) Act 2020 (c.1) which received Royal Assent on 23 January 2020

25

125 Subsection (4) of new section 7B directs the reader to look also at the specific parts of the Act which give specific further legislative effect to other relevant parts of the EEA EFTA Separation Agreement and the Swiss Citizens' Rights Agreements also covered by section 6 - namely, citizens' rights, interpretation of law relating to the EEA EFTA Separation Agreement and the Swiss Citizens' Rights Agreement, power in connection with certain EU and EEA separation issues, and powers involving the devolved authorities in connection with certain EU and EEA separation issues. This list is not definitive, and the reader should look to all pieces of legislation which may be relevant, when seeking to clarify what section 6 applies to.

126 Subsection (5) defines 'the relevant EEA states' as Norway, Iceland and Liechtenstein.

127 Subsection (6) provides definitions for the EEA EFTA Separation Agreement and the Swiss Citizens' Rights Agreement.

Section 7: Rights related to residence: application deadline and temporary protection

128 This section provides Ministers of the Crown with a power to make regulations implementing the provisions in the Agreements which enable the UK to require individuals within scope of the Agreements or within scope of residence scheme immigration rules (the protected cohort) to apply for a UK immigration status (leave to enter or remain) conferring their residence rights under those Agreements by a specific deadline. It also enables regulations to be made that ensure that the protected cohort continue to enjoy the residence rights in the UK pending conferral of their new immigration status. The UK is giving effect to its commitments in the Agreements regarding residence status for EU citizens, EEA EFTA and Swiss nationals and their family members through the EU Settlement Scheme, which was established under Immigration Rules made under section 3(2) of the Immigration Act 1971.

129 Free movement rights for EU citizens and EEA EFTA nationals are set out in the EU Treaties and Directive 2004/38/EC and implemented domestically through section 7 of the Immigration Act 1988 and the EEA Regulations 2016. Free movement rights for Swiss nationals are set out in the FMOPA (as defined above), and also implemented domestically through the EEA Regulations 2016. In line with government policy, the Home Office will seek parliamentary approval to, at the end of the implementation period, end the UK's participation in the free movement of people within the European Economic Area through the planned Immigration and Social Security Co-ordination (EU Withdrawal) Act. By ending free movement, EU citizens, EEA EFTA nationals, and Swiss nationals will become subject to immigration control. Once free movement has ended, beneficiaries of the citizens' rights part of the Agreements who have not yet secured leave to enter or remain in the UK under the EU Settlement Scheme would no longer have a lawful basis to reside in the UK unless further provision is made.

130 Subsection (1)(a) enables a Minister of the Crown to specify the deadline for applications for immigration status under the EU Settlement Scheme, as set out in Article 18(1)(b) of the Withdrawal Agreement, Article 17(1)(b) of the EEA EFTA Separation Agreement, and Article 16(1)(b) of the Swiss Citizens' Rights Agreement. As provided for in the Agreements, this deadline must not be less than six months from the end of the implementation period. This provides for a grace period after the end of the implementation period in which EU law will no longer apply but the rights and protections flowing from the Agreements must be available in legal and practical terms to individuals under the Agreements and members of the protected cohort who have not yet obtained their immigration status under domestic law.

131 The powers under this section may also be used to give effect to amendments to the Withdrawal Agreement, and the EEA EFTA Separation Agreement adopted by the Joint Committee falling within the scope of the matters provided for by this section.

These Explanatory Notes relate to the European Union (Withdrawal Agreement) Act 2020 (c.1) which received Royal Assent on 23 January 2020

26

132 Subsection (1)(b), (c) and (d) enables a Minister of the Crown, by regulations, to implement Article 18(2) of the Withdrawal Agreement, Article 17(2) of the EEA EFTA Separation Agreement, and Article 16(2) of the Swiss Citizens' Rights Agreement. Those provisions apply all the rights provided for in the citizens' rights parts of the Agreements to members of the protected cohort who have not yet obtained their immigration status under domestic law during the grace period.

133 Subsection (1)(e), (f) and (g) enable a Minister of the Crown to make regulations to provide that, where a person has made a valid application for immigration status under the EU Settlement Scheme, all the rights provided for in the citizens' rights parts of the Agreements shall apply to that person until the application is finally determined, including procedures for judicial redress where applicable.

134 The Government intends that regulations under subsection (1)(b) to (g) will give effect to the relevant provisions in the Agreements largely by saving the necessary components of the existing regime in the EEA Regulations 2016 that protect the rights of EU citizens, EEA EFTA nationals, under the Free Movement Directive and Swiss nationals under Annex I of FMOPA during the grace period and pending resolution of individual applications for status under the EU Settlement Scheme.

135 Subsections (2) and (3) will enable regulations under subsection (1) to apply both to the persons whom the provision in question applies and to all those who are eligible for or in the case of subsection (3) have applied for leave under the EU Settlement Scheme. This will enable provision to be made, for example, to protect the position of certain groups who currently derive their residence rights from EU law, but who are not covered by the Agreements such as family members of British citizens who benefit from the *Surinder Singh* principle.[6]

136 Subsection (4) states that regulations made under this power may modify any provision made by or under an enactment.

Section 8: Frontier workers

137 This section provides Ministers of the Crown with powers to make regulations to put in place protections to the rights of EU, EEA EFTA and Swiss frontier workers who are economically active in, but not resident in, the UK at the end of the implementation period, and the ability to establish a permit scheme enabling the issuance of documents to frontier workers. This section may also be used to give effect to amendments to the Withdrawal Agreement and the EEA EFTA Separation Agreement adopted by the Joint Committee falling within the scope of the matters provided for by this section.

138 Under the Common Travel Area (CTA), UK and Irish citizens will have the right to move freely and work across the Irish border, and so will not need to rely on these frontier worker rights. A Memorandum of Understanding between the UK and Ireland on the Common Travel Area was signed between the UK Government and the Irish Government on 8 May 2019. The Memorandum of Understanding is clear that the national laws of the UK and Ireland will continue to provide for the right to work afforded to British citizens in Ireland and Irish citizens in the UK.

---

[6] *Surinder Singh* established the principle that nationals of Member States should not be deterred from leaving their country of origin to pursue an economic activity in another Member State. They would be so deterred if on returning to the Member State of which they are a national they did not enjoy conditions at least equivalent to those they would enjoy under community law in the territory of another Member State. In this case in respect of family reunification rights.

These Explanatory Notes relate to the European Union (Withdrawal Agreement) Act 2020 (c.1) which received Royal Assent on 23 January 2020

27

139 This power may also be used to give effect to amendments to the Withdrawal Agreement, and the EEA EFTA Separation Agreement, adopted by the Joint Committee falling within the scope of the matters provided for by this section.

140 Subsection (1) provides Ministers of the Crown with a power to make regulations for the purpose of implementing Articles 24(3) and 25(3) of the Withdrawal Agreement, Articles 23(3) and 24(3) of the EEA EFTA Separation Agreement, and Article 20(2) of the Swiss Citizens' Rights Agreement, concerning rights of employed and self-employed frontier workers to enter their state of work, and retention of the rights that they enjoyed as workers there before the end of the implementation period.

141 Subsection (2) provides Ministers of the Crown with a power to make regulations for the purpose of implementing Article 26 of the Withdrawal Agreement, Article 25 of the EEA EFTA Separation Agreement, and Articles 21(1)(a) and 21(2) of the Swiss Citizens' Rights Agreement. These provisions allow for a permit system to certify EU citizens, EEA EFTA and Swiss nationals as frontier workers in the UK at the end of the implementation period.

142 Subsection (3) states that the power to make regulations under this section may be made by modifying the Immigration Acts, as defined in Schedule 1 of the Interpretation Act 1978[7], including secondary legislation made under those Acts, or any other secondary legislation.

Section 9: Restrictions on rights of entry and residence

143 This section provides Ministers of the Crown with a power to make regulations to implement provisions of the Agreements that relate to restrictions on rights of entry and residence. Article 20(1), (3), and (4) of the Withdrawal Agreement, Article 19(1), (3), and (4) of the EEA EFTA Separation Agreement, and Articles 17(1), 17(3), and 20(3) of the Swiss Citizens' Rights Agreement outline the conditions for restrictions on rights of entry and residence in relation to protected persons.

144 These articles provide that the restriction of a protected person's entry or residence rights on the grounds of conduct committed before the end of the implementation period must be made in accordance with Chapter VI of Directive 2004/83/EC, and Article 5 of Annex I of the FMOPA. These articles also provide that protected persons can continue to be removed from the UK as a result of fraud and/or abuse of their rights, as is currently the case under the EEA Regulations 2016.

145 This power may, among other things, be exercised by saving and modifying the current provisions for restricting admission and residence rights under the EEA Regulations 2016, to ensure that those provisions continue to apply in relation to restriction decisions made on the grounds of conduct taking place before the end of the implementation period. Specifically, where restriction decisions are made on the grounds of conduct that took place before the end of the implementation period, the public policy, public security or public health test will apply. The power may also be used to save and modify provisions within the EEA Regulations 2016 relating to the removal of EEA nationals and their family members on the grounds of fraud or abuse of their rights.

146 This power may additionally be used to give effect to amendments to the Withdrawal Agreement, and the EEA EFTA Separation Agreement adopted by the Joint Committee falling within the scope of the matters provided for by this section.

---

[7] Schedule 1 of the Interpretation Act 1978 states that the 'Immigration Acts' has the meaning given by section 61(2) of the UK Borders Act 2007.

These Explanatory Notes relate to the European Union (Withdrawal Agreement) Act 2020 (c.1) which received Royal Assent on 23 January 2020

28

147 Subsection (1) provides for the power to make regulations to implement Article 20(1), (3), and (4) of the Withdrawal Agreement, and the corresponding Article 19(1), (3), and (4) of the EEA EFTA Separation Agreement, and Articles 17(1), 17(3), and 20(3) of the Swiss Citizens' Rights Agreement.

148 Subsection (2) provides that regulations under subsection (1) can be applied both to persons to whom the provisions set out in subsection (1) apply and those not so covered but granted leave to enter or remain under residence scheme immigration rules, those who have entry clearance granted by virtue of relevant entry clearance immigration rules, and those who otherwise have leave to enter granted after arriving with entry clearance by virtue of relevant entry clearance immigration rules.

149 Subsection (3) states that references to a person who has entry clearance or leave to enter or remain include persons who would have had entry clearance or leave to enter or remain but for the making of a deportation order under section 5(1) of the Immigration Act 1971 or any other decision made in connection with restricting a right to enter the UK.

150 Subsection (4) states that the power to make regulations under this section may be made by modifying the Immigration Acts, as defined in Schedule 1 of the Interpretation Act 1978, including secondary legislation made under those Acts or by modifying provisions made under any other primary legislation.

Section 10: Retention of existing grounds for deportation

151 This section ensures that the deportation provisions within the Immigration Act 1971 must be exercised in a way that is compatible with the Agreements. This means that the domestic threshold for the deportation of third country nationals (that is, on the grounds that deportation is conducive to the public good or following the recommendation of a court) will not apply to EU citizens, EEA EFTA and Swiss nationals, and their family members who are protected by the Agreements or by the UK's domestic implementation of the Agreements where the decision relates to conduct taking place before the end of the implementation period. The section also creates an exception to the automatic deportation regime within the UK Borders Act 2007 (under which an individual must be deported if they are convicted of an offence with a custodial sentence of 12 months or more, unless certain exceptions apply) for persons protected by the Agreements or by the UK's domestic implementation of the Agreements where the offence that would have justified deportation consisted of or included conduct that took place before the end of the implementation period.

152 As set out above, Article 20 of the Withdrawal Agreement, Article 19 of the EEA EFTA Separation Agreement, and Articles 17 and 20 of the Swiss Citizens' Rights Agreement provide that any conduct committed by persons protected by the Agreements prior to the end of the implementation period must be considered in accordance with Chapter VI of Directive 2004/38/EC, and Article 5 of Annex 1 of the FMOPA. This means that the EEA public policy, public security or public health test must be applied to conduct committed before the end of the implementation period for the purposes of taking deportation decisions, rather than the domestic provisions at section 3(5) and 3(6) of the Immigration Act 1971 (that is, that the deportation is conducive to the public good or following the recommendation of a court).

These Explanatory Notes relate to the European Union (Withdrawal Agreement) Act 2020 (c.1) which received Royal Assent on 23 January 2020

29

153 Under Chapter VI of Directive 2004/38/EC, as implemented by the EEA Regulations 2016, when assessing whether the public policy, public security or public health test has been met there are a number of criteria that must be considered, including, in the case of public policy or public security, whether the individual's conduct poses a genuine, present and sufficiently serious threat to one of the fundamental interests of society in the UK. The threshold to be met increases depending on length of residence and age. Deportation needs to be justified on 'serious grounds of public policy or public security' where they have permanent residence; or on 'imperative grounds of public security' where they are an EEA national who has been resident for over ten years or are under the age of 18, in the latter case unless the decision is in their best interests. The threshold for deporting an EEA national is, therefore, higher than that applied to third country nationals under section 3(5) Immigration Act 1971 or following the recommendation of a court under section 3(6) Immigration Act 1971 who are not exercising any EEA rights. This section ensures that protected persons continue to benefit from the EU law thresholds where the conduct justifying the restriction took place before the end of the implementation period.

154 Subsections (1) to (4) of this section amend section 3 of the Immigration Act 1971. In particular:

  a. subsection (2) inserts a new subsection (5A) into section 3 of the Immigration Act 1971 providing that a relevant person's deportation may not be considered conducive to the public good if that deportation would be in breach of the UK's obligations under the Agreements; or in the case of persons who are not technically protected by the Agreements but who are relevant persons, the deportation would be in breach of the Agreements if the Agreements applied to them;

  b. subsection (3) inserts a new subsection (6A) into section 3 of the Immigration Act 1971 preventing a court from recommending deportation of a relevant person if the offence for which they were convicted consisted of or included conduct committed before the end of the implementation period;

  c. subsection (4) inserts new subsections (10) and (11) into section 3 of the Immigration Act 1971:

      i. the new subsection (10) defines a 'relevant person'. A relevant person includes anyone who has been granted leave to enter or remain under residence scheme immigration rules, anyone in the UK having arrived with entry clearance granted by virtue of relevant entry clearance immigration rules, frontier workers, and those who may be granted leave to enter or remain for a course of planned healthcare treatment; and

      ii. the new subsection (11) ensures that certain definitions contained within the European Union (Withdrawal Agreement) Act 2020 apply for the purposes of section 3 of the Immigration Act 1971, as amended by the Act.

155 Subsection (5) inserts multiple new subsections into section 33 of the UK Borders Act 2007. In particular, it inserts:

  a. a new subsection (6B), which creates a new exception to automatic deportation for relevant persons, where the offence for which the relevant person was convicted consisted of or included conduct that took place before the end of the implementation period;

  b. a new subsection (6C), which defines a 'relevant person' in the same way as subsection 4 of this section provides;

These Explanatory Notes relate to the European Union (Withdrawal Agreement) Act 2020 (c.1) which received Royal Assent on 23 January 2020

30

    c.   a new subsection (6D), which ensures that certain definitions contained within the European Union (Withdrawal Agreement) Act 2020 apply for the purposes of section 33 of the UK Borders Act 2007.

156 Subsection (6) clarifies the meaning of references to having leave to enter or remain in the United Kingdom in section 3(10) of the Immigration Act 1971 and section 33(6C) of the UK Borders Act 2007, which are inserted by this section, making clear that they include leave granted by virtue of those rules before section 17 of this Act comes into force.

Section 11: Appeals etc against citizens' rights immigration decisions

157 Articles 18 and 21 of the Withdrawal Agreement, and Articles 17 and 20 of the EEA EFTA Separation Agreement, provide for a right of judicial redress against decisions refusing to grant residence status under the EU Settlement Scheme, or to restrict residence rights.

158 The effect of Article 20 of the Withdrawal Agreement, and Article 19 of the EEA EFTA Separation Agreement, is to provide for a right of judicial redress against restrictions on rights of entry to the UK for frontier workers and those continuing a course of planned healthcare treatment.

159 Article 8 of the Swiss Citizens' Rights Agreement provides for similar rights of judicial redress.

160 This section provides a Minister of the Crown with a power to make regulations to make provision for, or in connection with, appeals against:

    a.   a decision made in connection with entry clearance by virtue of relevant entry clearance immigration rules;

    b.   a decision made in connection with leave to enter or remain by virtue of residence scheme immigration rules;

    c.   a decision made in connection with entry clearance for the purposes of acquiring leave to enter or remain in relation to a healthcare right of entry;

    d.   a decision made in connection with leave to enter or remain in relation to a healthcare right of entry;

    e.   a decision made in connection with a right to enter or remain by virtue of regulations for frontier workers;

    f.   a decision to make, or a refusal to revoke a deportation order under section 5(1) of the Immigration Act 1971 in relation to a relevant person; and

    g.   any other decision made in connection with restricting the right of a relevant person to enter the United Kingdom (citizens' rights immigration decisions).

161 This power may also be used to make provision for, or in connection with, reviews (including judicial reviews) of decisions within point g above.

162 Furthermore, it may be used to give effect to amendments to the Withdrawal Agreement and the EEA EFTA Separation Agreement adopted by the Joint Committee falling within the scope of the matters provided for by this section.

163 Subsection (1) states that a Minister of the Crown may make regulations to make provision for, or in connection with, appeals against citizens' rights immigration decisions.

164 Subsection (2) defines 'citizens' rights immigration decisions' in connection with which a Minister of the Crown may make appeals regulations under this section.

These Explanatory Notes relate to the European Union (Withdrawal Agreement) Act 2020 (c.1) which received Royal Assent on 23 January 2020

31

165 Subsection (3) states that a Minister of the Crown may make regulations to make provision for, or in connection with, reviews (including judicial reviews) of decisions within subsection (2)(g).

166 Subsection (4) states that the power to make regulations under this subsection (1) or (3) may, among other things, be exercised by modifying any provision made by or under an enactment. Subsection (5) gives an example of this providing that regulations made under the power may, for example, apply with or without modifications any enactment which applies in relation to appeals under section 82 of the Nationality, Immigration and Asylum Act 2002 or section 2 of the Special Immigration Appeals Commission Act 1997. This power will be used, for example, to provide for certification of appeals including on national security grounds.

167 Subsection (6) defines a 'healthcare right of entry' for the purposes of subsection (2) as a right to enter the UK that a person has by virtue of Article 32(1)(b) of the Withdrawal Agreement, Article 31(1)(b) of the EEA EFTA Separation Agreement, or Article 26a(1)(b) of the Swiss Citizens' Rights Agreement.

168 Subsection (7) defines a 'relevant person' for the purposes of subsection (2)(f) and (g) as a person to whom Article 20 of the Withdrawal Agreement, Article 19 of the EEA EFTA Separation Agreement, or Articles 17 or 20(3) of the Swiss Citizens' Rights Agreement applies, or, if they do not fall within these Articles, a person who has entry clearance granted by virtue of relevant entry clearance immigration rules, has leave to enter or remain granted by virtue of residence scheme immigration rules or otherwise has leave to enter granted after arriving with entry clearance granted by virtue of relevant entry clearance immigration rules.

169 Subsection (8) states that references in subsection (7)(b) to a person who has entry clearance or leave to enter or remain include references to a person who would have had entry clearance or leave to enter or remain but for the making of a deportation order under section 5(1) of the Immigration Act 1971 or any other decision made in connection with restricting the right of the person to enter the UK.

170 Appeal rights set up under this power will be to the First-tier Tribunal (Immigration and Asylum Chamber) with an onward right of appeal with permission to the Upper Tribunal on a point of law.

171 The Immigration and Asylum Chamber currently hears appeals in respect of protection and human rights claims and appeals under the EEA Regulations 2016. The procedure for residence scheme appeals (including the time limits for appealing) will be covered by the Tribunal Procedure Rules. The Tribunal Procedure Rules set out the rules of procedure of the First-tier Tribunal, including service of documents, the procedure for summoning witnesses, how the Tribunal may receive evidence, and other such procedural matters.

Section 12: Recognition of professional qualifications

172 This section gives Ministers of the Crown and the devolved authorities the power to make necessary regulations to implement:

   a. Chapter 3 (Professional Qualifications) of Title II of Part 2 of the Withdrawal Agreement;

   b. Chapter 3 (Professional Qualifications) of Title II of Part 2 of the EEA EFTA Separation Agreement; and

   c. Article 23(4) (so far as relates to recognition of professional qualifications) and Part 4 (Mutual Recognition of Professional Qualifications) of the Swiss Citizens' Rights Agreement.

These Explanatory Notes relate to the European Union (Withdrawal Agreement) Act 2020 (c.1) which received Royal Assent on 23 January 2020

32

173 The provisions in the Agreements set out that professional qualifications held by EU citizens and EEA EFTA nationals, who are resident or frontier working in the UK by the end of the implementation period, and recognised, or in the process of being recognised, by a UK professional regulator before the end of the implementation period, will continue to be recognised. Family members of EU citizens and EEA EFTA nationals who are resident in the UK will also have rights to have their qualifications recognised under these agreements.

174 Under the Swiss Citizens' Rights Agreement, Swiss nationals who have had qualifications recognised or applied for recognition before the end of the implementation period will continue to have their qualifications recognised. Swiss nationals will have an additional four years from the end of the implementation period to make applications for recognition, so long as the individual has obtained, or was in the process of obtaining, a qualification before the end of the implementation period.

175 All persons with recognised qualifications under the Agreements will be entitled to practice the profession under the same conditions as UK nationals.

176 For the purpose of this section, the devolved authorities are the Scottish Ministers, the Welsh Ministers and a Northern Ireland department.

177 For EU citizens and EEA EFTA nationals, this section applies to recognition decisions made under UK legislation that implements the following EU directives:

    a. Title III of Directive 2005/36/EC - right to practice a regulated profession based on the recognition of professional qualifications or professional experience gained in another EEA state;

    b. Article 10(1) and (3) of Directive 98/5/EC - admission to the profession of lawyer in another EEA state;

    c. Article 14 of Directive 2006/43/EC - approval of statutory auditors from another EEA state; and

    d. Council Directive 74/556/EEC - recognition of knowledge and ability needed to engage in the trade and distribution of toxic products.

178 For Swiss nationals, this section applies to decisions made under UK legislation that implements the following EU directives:

    a. Title III of Directive 2005/36/EC – right to practice a regulated profession based on the recognition of professional qualifications or professional experience gained in another EEA state;

    b. Directive 98/5/EC - admission to the profession of lawyer in another EEA state;

    c. Council Directive 77/249/EEC - to facilitate the effective exercise by lawyers of freedom to provide services;

    d. Council Directive 74/556/EEC - recognition of knowledge and ability needed to engage in the trade and distribution of toxic products; and

    e. Council Directive 86/653/EEC in respect of self-employed commercial agents.

These Explanatory Notes relate to the European Union (Withdrawal Agreement) Act 2020 (c.1) which received Royal Assent on 23 January 2020

33

179 The recognition of professional qualifications provisions in the Withdrawal Agreement and EEA Separation Agreement only apply for the purposes of establishment, and not for the temporary and occasional provision of services. The Swiss Citizens' Rights Agreement also makes provision for the purposes of establishment. In addition, Article 23 of the Swiss Citizens' Rights Agreement provides that those providing services on a temporary basis from Switzerland to the UK or from the UK to Switzerland shall have the right to continue to do so after the end of the implementation period, provided certain conditions are met. Those in the scope of Article 23 may continue to rely upon the Council Directive 77/249/EEC, which facilitates the exercise by lawyers of freedom to provide services, and the provisions of Title II of Directive 2005/36/EC, which concerns the freedom to provide services for other regulated professions.

180 This power may also be used to give effect to amendments to the Withdrawal Agreement, and the EEA EFTA Separation Agreement, adopted by the Joint Committee falling within the scope of the matters provided for by this section.

181 Subsection (1) provides that the power may be made to make regulations to implement Chapter 3 of Title II of Part 2 of the Withdrawal Agreement, as well as to supplement the effect of section 7A of the EU (Withdrawal) Act 2018 in relation to that Chapter, and to deal with matters arising out of, or related to, that Chapter.

182 Subsection (2) provides that the power may be made to make regulations to implement Chapter 3 of Title II of Part 2 of the EEA EFTA Separation Agreement, as well as to supplement the effect of section 7B of the EU (Withdrawal) Act 2018 in relation to that Chapter, and to deal with matters arising out of, or related to, that Chapter.

183 Subsection (3) provides that the power may be made to make regulations to implement Article 23(4) (so far as relates to recognition of professional qualifications) and Part 4 of the Swiss Citizens' Rights Agreement, as well as to supplement the effect of section 7B of the EU (Withdrawal) Act 2018 in relation to those provisions, and to deal with matters arising out of, or related to, those provisions. Article 23(4) sets out that Swiss service providers, providing temporary and occasional services in regulated professions in accordance with Article 23(1) can continue to do so.

184 Subsection (4) outlines that for the purposes of subsection (3) the professional qualification provisions of the Swiss Citizens' Rights Agreement are Part 4 and Article 23(4) (so far as it relates to the recognition of professional qualifications).

185 Subsection (5) provides that an appropriate authority may make the regulations that apply not only to persons within the scope of the relevant provisions of the Withdrawal Agreement and EEA EFTA Separation Agreement but also to persons outside the scope of those agreements who have been granted leave to enter or remain in the United Kingdom under the residence scheme immigration rules (the protected cohort) (see section 17).

186 Subsection (6) provides that the powers in subsections (1), (2) and (3) may be used to modify any provision made by or under an enactment but subsection (7) provides that primary legislation passed made after IP completion day is not caught by subsection (6).

187 Subsection (8) defines an 'appropriate authority' for the purpose of this section as meaning a Minister of the Crown, a devolved authority or a Minister of the Crown acting jointly with a devolved authority.

188 Subsection (9) references Schedule 1 which makes further provision concerning the powers of the devolved authorities to make regulations under this section.

These Explanatory Notes relate to the European Union (Withdrawal Agreement) Act 2020 (c.1) which received Royal Assent on 23 January 2020

34

Section 13: Co-ordination of social security systems

189 The EU Social Security Co-ordination Regulations[8] protect the social security position of persons who move and work around the EU. The Regulations coordinate the application of different Member States' social security systems to avoid conflict or duplication, as well as providing for aggregation of periods of work, insurance (National Insurance contributions in the UK) or residence to help meet benefit entitlement conditions and for the payment of certain benefits to or in respect of a person living in another Member State ('export' of benefits). Individuals within scope will continue to benefit from co-ordination rules as set out in the Agreements.

190 These rules ensure that a worker (and their employer) or a self-employed worker only pay contributions into one Member State's social security scheme at a time and determine which Member State is responsible for the payment of benefits and the cost of healthcare. They set out certain rights to healthcare cover in the UK, reimbursed by the Member State responsible for that cover, and equivalent rights for healthcare cover in Member States, reimbursed by the UK.

191 The EU Social Security Co-ordination Regulations will apply directly to those within scope of Title III of Part 2 of the Withdrawal Agreement by virtue of section 5. They will also apply directly to those within scope of Title III of Part 2 of the EEA EFTA Separation Agreement and Part 3 of the Swiss Citizen's Rights Agreement by virtue of section 6. Future updates to these Regulations, where added to an Annex of the Agreements under a Joint Committee mechanism, will also apply directly.

192 Section 13 provides Ministers of the Crown or a devolved authority (separately or jointly) with a power to implement these sections of the Agreements and supplement the effect of the Agreements as applied in domestic law and any matters which arise out of this, for example to remedy any unforeseen inconsistencies with domestic legislation.

193 This power will also be available in relation to future changes to the EU Social Security Co-ordination Regulations that are added to the Agreements and so take effect in domestic law directly by virtue of sections 5 and 6. This will ensure that the UK can react to future changes and continue to meet its obligations under the Agreements.

194 The power may also be used to make changes to administrative and operational systems that implement the co-ordination of social security systems domestically. This could include, for example, providing for the sharing of data either with other states or between appropriate authorities in the UK, where it is necessary to give full effect to the Agreements (should provision be needed beyond the data sharing articles of the EU Social Security Co-ordination Regulations).

195 The power also enables a Minister or a devolved authority to supplement the effect of Article 7A of the EU (Withdrawal) Act 2018 in relation to Title III of Part 2 of the Withdrawal Agreement. Subsections (2) and (3) allow equivalent provision to be made in respect of Article 7B of the EU (Withdrawal) Act 2018 in relation to Title III of Part 2 of the EEA EFTA Separation Agreement and Article 23(4) and Part 3 of the Swiss Citizens' Rights Agreement.

196 This power may also be used to give effect to amendments to the Withdrawal Agreement, and the EEA EFTA Separation Agreement, adopted by the Joint Committee falling within the scope of the matters provided for by this section.

---

[8] Regulations (EC) 883/2004 and 987/2009, and Regulations (EEC) 1408/71 and 574/72 in respect of third country nationals.

These Explanatory Notes relate to the European Union (Withdrawal Agreement) Act 2020 (c.1) which received Royal Assent on 23 January 2020

35

197 Subsection (4) defines the social security co-ordination provisions in the Swiss Citizens' Rights Agreement.

198 Subsection (5) states that the power to make regulations may be used to modify any provision made under an enactment.

199 Subsection (6) defines 'appropriate authority' for the purposes of this section. Subsection (7) references Schedule 1 which makes further provision concerning the powers of the devolved authorities.

Section 14: Non-discrimination, equal treatment and rights of workers etc.

200 The Agreements provide for the protection of rights to equal treatment and non-discrimination for the protected cohort and frontier workers (as defined in section 8). The non-discrimination, equal treatment and rights of workers power allows for provision to be made to ensure that domestic legislation is not inconsistent with these rights under the Agreements.

201 This section provides Ministers of the Crown and the devolved authorities with a power to implement the equal treatment provisions in the Agreements, including ensuring that domestic legislation is consistent with these provisions. Subsection (1) restricts the scope of this power to implementing Articles 12, 23, 24(1), 25(1), 24(3) and 25(3) of the Withdrawal Agreement. Subsection (2) provides that the power may be used to implement Articles 11, 22, 23(1), 24(1), 23(3) and 24(3) in the EEA EFTA Separation Agreement. Subsection (3) provides that the power may be used to implement Articles 7, 18, 19, 20(1) and 23(1) in the Swiss Citizens' Rights Agreement.

202 This power may also be used to give effect to amendments to the Withdrawal Agreement, and the EEA EFTA Separation Agreement adopted by the Joint Committee falling within the scope of the matters provided for by this section.

203 Subsection (4) provides that regulations made under subsections (1), (2) and (3) may be made so as to apply both to persons who are covered by the relevant Articles of the Agreements, as well as persons to whom the provision in question does not apply but who may be granted leave to remain under the residence scheme immigration rules, whether or not they have been granted such leave.

204 Regulations made under this section may be used, for example, to provide that EU citizens, EEA EFTA nationals and Swiss nationals with pre-existing access to benefits and services maintain the same access to benefits and services as they were entitled to under EU law before the end of the implementation period.

205 Under current rules, access to publicly funded benefits and services for EU citizens and EEA EFTA nationals and their family members may be linked to their status under the EEA Regulations 2016. Those with permanent residence under these Regulations are entitled to benefits and services on the same terms as UK nationals, subject to meeting the relevant eligibility criteria.

206 Where an individual does not have permanent residence, entitlement to these benefits and services is subject to eligibility tests. Eligibility may be linked to holding another status under domestic law, for example being a 'qualifying person' under the EEA Regulations 2016 (for example, a worker in genuine and effective employment). This power will be used to save the operation of the EEA Regulations 2016 and related domestic law for the purpose of preserving access to benefits and services based on the same conditions as now.

207 Subsection (5) states that the power to make regulations may be used to modify any provision made under an enactment.

These Explanatory Notes relate to the European Union (Withdrawal Agreement) Act 2020 (c.1) which received Royal Assent on 23 January 2020

36

208 Subsection (6) defines 'appropriate authority' for the purposes of this section. Subsection (7) references Schedule 1 which makes further provision concerning the powers of the devolved authorities in respect of citizens' rights provisions.

Section 15: Independent Monitoring Authority for the Citizens' Rights Agreements

209 This section establishes an independent authority to monitor the implementation and application of Part 2 of the Withdrawal Agreement, and Part 2 of the EEA EFTA Separation Agreement.

210 Establishment of this authority is required to implement Article 159 of the Withdrawal Agreement, and Article 64 of the EEA EFTA Separation Agreement.

211 Subsection (1) establishes the body as the Independent Monitoring Authority for the Citizens' Rights Agreements. Subsection (2) sets out the abbreviation of 'IMA'.

212 Subsection (3) references Schedule 2, which contains provisions about the IMA's constitution, the IMA's functions, functions of certain public authorities in relation to the IMA and the abolition of the IMA.

Section 16: Regulations: supplementary

213 Subsection (1) provides that in sections 7, 8, 9 and 14, a power to make provision for the purpose of implementing an Article or Chapter or Part of the Withdrawal Agreement, EEA EFTA Separation Agreement, or Swiss Citizens' Rights Agreement includes a power to make provision to supplement the effect of sections 7A and 7B of the EU (Withdrawal) Act 2018 in relation to that Article, Chapter, or Part.

214 Subsection (2) states that the conferral of a power on a Minister of the Crown in sections 7, 8, 9 or 11 does not affect the extent of any power of a devolved authority under sections 12, 13 or 14 which overlaps with a power under sections 7, 8, 9, or 11 by virtue of section 17(4).

215 Subsection (3) states that regulations made under the citizens' rights provisions may not provide for the conferral of functions or the delegation of functions to a person who is not a public authority.

216 Subsection (4) defines a public authority under subsection (3) as a person carrying out functions of a public nature.

Section 17: Interpretation: Part 3

217 This section provides definitions for terms used in Part 3 (citizens' rights) of the Act.

218 Subsection (1) sets out the definition for 'residence scheme immigration rules'.

219 Subsection (2) sets out the definition for 'relevant entry clearance immigration rules'.

220 Subsection (3) provides that references to having leave to enter or remain in the UK by virtue of the residence scheme immigration rules (which provide for the protected cohort) includes leave granted by virtue of those rules before the citizens' rights provisions in the Act come into force.

221 Subsection (4) states that a reference to a Chapter, Title or Part or other provision of the Withdrawal Agreement, the EEA EFTA Separation Agreement or the Swiss Citizens' Rights Agreements in the citizens' rights provisions of the Act includes a reference to any other provision in the Withdrawal Agreement, the EEA EFTA Separation Agreement, or the Swiss Citizens' Rights Agreement that relates to that provision , as well as any provision of EU law which is applied by or referred to in that Chapter, Title, Part or other provision.

222 Subsection (5) sets out the definitions of 'entry clearance', and 'immigration rules'.

These Explanatory Notes relate to the European Union (Withdrawal Agreement) Act 2020 (c.1) which received Royal Assent on 23 January 2020

37

Section 18: Main power in connection with other separation issues

223 This section, inserted as new section 8B of the EU (Withdrawal) Act 2018, provides Ministers of the Crown with a power to implement the Other Separation Issues, which form Part 3 of the Withdrawal Agreement and Part 3 of the EEA EFTA Separation Agreement. Ministers can only use this power in connection with those Parts. It is designed to enable implementation of the Other Separation Issues in domestic law and to supplement the effect of new section 7A and new section 7B.

224 Subsection (1) provides Ministers with the power to make legislative changes which they consider appropriate for the purposes of implementing Part 3 of the Withdrawal Agreement. This includes supplementing the effect of the new section 7A of the EU (Withdrawal) Act 2018 in relation to Part 3, or dealing with matters arising out of, or related to, Part 3. This includes giving effect to amendments to the Withdrawal Agreement adopted by the Joint Committee in relation to Part 3.

225 Subsection (2) provides Ministers with an equivalent power to make legislative changes which they consider appropriate for the purposes of implementing Part 3 of the EEA EFTA Separation Agreement. This includes supplementing the effect of the new section 7B of the EU (Withdrawal) Act 2018 in relation to Part 3, or dealing with matters arising out of, or related to, Part 3.

226 Subsection (3) provides that secondary legislation made under this power is capable of doing anything an Act of Parliament can do, subject to the restrictions specified in subsection (5).

227 Subsection (4) clarifies that the power can be used to restate elements of Part 3 of the Withdrawal Agreement and of the EEA EFTA Separation Agreement that automatically become domestic law via the new section 7A and 7B. This type of restatement can be made where it would be helpful to provide clarity or to make the law more accessible.

228 Subsection (5) places a series of restrictions on the power, stating what it cannot do. The power cannot be used to impose or increase taxation or fees, make retrospective provision, create a relevant criminal offence, establish a public authority, amend, repeal or revoke the Human Rights Act 1998 (nor legislation made under it), or amend or repeal the Scotland Act 1998, the Government of Wales Act 2006 or the Northern Ireland Act 1998 (unless the regulations are made by virtue of paragraph 21(b) of Schedule 7 to the EU (Withdrawal) Act 2018 or are amending or repealing any provision of those Acts which modifies another enactment).

229 Subsection (6) defines references to Part 3 of the Withdrawal Agreement and of the EEA EFTA Separation Agreement as including references to any provisions of EU law applied by or referred to in that Part.

230 The scrutiny procedures for this power are set out in Schedule 4.

Section 19: Powers corresponding to section 18 involving devolved authorities

231 A new Part 1B inserted into Schedule 2 of the EU (Withdrawal) Act 2018 provides a corresponding power for the devolved authorities to implement Part 3 of the Withdrawal Agreement and of the EEA EFTA Separation Agreement. New paragraph 11G, subsections (1) to (4), set out that this power can be used by devolved authorities acting alone, or by Ministers of the Crown and devolved authorities acting jointly.

232 This power can be used for the same purposes as the power at new section 8B and the same restrictions apply, subject to paragraphs 11H and 11I.

These Explanatory Notes relate to the European Union (Withdrawal Agreement) Act 2020 (c.1) which received Royal Assent on 23 January 2020

233 Paragraph 11H provides that the power to implement Part 3 of the Withdrawal Agreement and of the EEA EFTA Separation Agreement cannot be used outside of devolved competence, as defined in paragraphs 11J to 11L, where exercised by devolved authorities acting alone.

234 Paragraph 11I provides that, where a devolved authority is making a provision for the purposes of implementing Part 3 of the Withdrawal Agreement or of the EEA EFTA Separation Agreement, the requirements for consent, joint exercise or consultation with the UK Government will apply where the type of provision would otherwise require UK Government consent, consultation or joint exercise of powers.

Section 20: Financial provision

235 This section is necessary to allow for payments to be made to the EU for the purposes of complying with any Withdrawal Agreement obligations.

236 Subsection (1) allows payments to be made from the Consolidated Fund (or from the National Loans Fund if so directed by the Treasury) for the purposes of complying with payment obligations provided for in the Withdrawal Agreement (i.e. all obligations under the Withdrawal Agreement to make payments to the EU or an EU entity, its institutions and projects). The authority to make payments is in the form of a standing service provision.

237 Subsection (2) provides that payments authorised under the standing service provision at subsection (1) will cease on 31 March 2021, with the exception of sums relating to the traditional own resources of the EU.

238 Subsection (3) requires that all sums due to the UK as a result of the Withdrawal Agreement (e.g. the reimbursement to the UK of the paid-in subscribed capital of the European Investment Bank) and received by a Minister of the Crown or a government department are to be paid into the Consolidated Fund, or if the Treasury so determines, the National Loans Fund. Sums received by other recipients (such as businesses, universities or local authorities) from the EU are not captured by this requirement.

239 Subsection (4) authorises expenditure by a Minister of the Crown, government department or devolved authority in anticipation of the exercise of a power to make subordinate legislation conferred or modified by or under the Act.

240 Subsection (5) is a general proposition that expenditure under the Act is to be paid out of money provided by Parliament, but does not itself authorise release of funds from the Consolidated Fund or National Loans Fund.

241 Subsection (6) clarifies that subsections (1), (3) and (5) are subject to other enactments. For example, payments required to fulfill the UK's obligations in relation to the European Development Fund, the European Union Emergency Trust Fund and the Facility for Refugees in Turkey will continue to be paid through a finance authority in the International Development Act 2002. Similarly, where other legislation makes specific provision that requires sums received to be handled differently, these provisions will prevail. Therefore, where EU Regulations applied by the Withdrawal Agreement (for example those governing the management of EU programmes such as the European Regional Development Fund) make specific provisions around the handling of receipts from the EU, these will continue.

242 Subsection (7) provides definitions of the terminology relevant to this section.

Section 21: Main power in connection with Ireland/Northern Ireland Protocol

243 This section provides Ministers of the Crown with the power to implement the Protocol on Ireland/Northern Ireland (hereafter 'the Protocol'). To that end, this section inserts a new section 8C into the EU (Withdrawal) Act 2018.

These Explanatory Notes relate to the European Union (Withdrawal Agreement) Act 2020 (c.1) which received Royal Assent on 23 January 2020

39

244 Subsection (1) of new section 8C confers a power on a Minister of the Crown to make legislative changes that they consider are appropriate for the purposes of implementing the Protocol. This includes supplementing the effect of the new section 7A of the EU (Withdrawal) Act 2018 (inserted by section 5 of this Act) in relation to the Protocol or dealing with matters arising out of, or related to, the Protocol. It also includes giving effect to amendments to the Withdrawal Agreement adopted by the Joint Committee falling within the scope of the particular matters that this power is intended to address.

245 Subsection (2) confirms that the power allows for the regulations made under subsection (1) to make any provision that could be made by an Act of Parliament, including modifying the EU (Withdrawal) Act 2018.

246 Subsection (3) clarifies that the power may be used to make provision facilitating the access of Northern Ireland goods to the market within Great Britain.

247 Subsection (4) clarifies that regulations made under subsection (3) may, among other things, provide for the recognition within Great Britain of technical regulations, assessments, registrations, certificates, approvals and authorisations issued by the authorities of a Member State or bodies established in a Member State in respect of Northern Ireland goods.

248 Subsection (5) clarifies that the power can be used to restate elements of the Protocol that automatically become domestic law via section 5 of this Act. This type of restatement can occur where it would be helpful to provide clarity or to make the law more accessible.

249 Subsection (6) contains a power enabling a Minister of the Crown to define, in regulations, the term 'qualifying Northern Ireland goods' for the purposes of the EU (Withdrawal) Act 2018.

250 Subsection (7) defines the Protocol for the purposes of the section as including any other provision of the Withdrawal Agreement so far as applying to the Protocol, and any provisions of EU law applied by, or referred to in the Protocol, but excludes the second sentence of Article 11(1) of the Protocol.

Section 22: Powers corresponding to section 21 involving devolved authorities

251 This section provides a corresponding power to that at section 21 allowing devolved authorities to make regulations to implement the Protocol in areas of devolved competence, inserting a new Part 1C into Schedule 2 to the EU (Withdrawal) Act 2018.

252 Paragraph 11M(1) provides devolved authorities with the power to make legislative changes which they consider appropriate for the purposes of implementing the Protocol. This includes supplementing the effect of section 7A of the EU (Withdrawal) Act 2018 (inserted by section 5 of the Act) in relation to the Protocol or dealing with matters arising out of, or related to, the Protocol. It also includes giving effect to amendments to the Withdrawal Agreement adopted by the Joint Committee falling within the scope of the particular matters that this power is intended to address.

253 Paragraph 11M(2) provides that this power can be used by a Minister of the Crown and a devolved administration acting jointly.

254 Paragraph 11M(3) provides that regulations made under this power are capable of doing anything an Act of Parliament can do.

255 Paragraph 11M(4) clarifies that the power may be used to make provision facilitating the access of Northern Ireland goods to the market within Great Britain.

These Explanatory Notes relate to the European Union (Withdrawal Agreement) Act 2020 (c.1) which received Royal Assent on 23 January 2020

40

256 Paragraph 11M(5) clarifies that regulations made under subsection (3) may, among other things, provide for the recognition within Great Britain of technical regulations, assessments, registrations, certificates, approvals and authorisations issued by the authorities of a Member State or bodies established in a Member State in respect of Northern Ireland goods.

257 Paragraph 11M(6) clarifies that the power can be used to restate elements of the Protocol that automatically become domestic law via section 5 of this Act. This type of restatement can occur where it would be helpful to provide clarity or to make the law more accessible.

258 Paragraph 11M(7) makes the use of this power subject to the provisions of paragraph 11N (restricting the power to being exercisable only in areas of devolved competence) and paragraph 11O (certain requirements for consent, joint exercise or consultation) of the same schedule of the EU (Withdrawal) Act 2018.

259 Paragraph 11M(8) defines the Protocol for the purposes of the section as including any other provision of the Withdrawal Agreement so far as applying to the Protocol, and any provisions of EU law applied by, or referred to in the Protocol, but excludes the second sentence of Article 11(1) of the Protocol.

260 Paragraph 11N provides that the power to implement the Protocol cannot be used outside of devolved competence, as defined in paragraphs 11P to 11R, where exercised by devolved authorities acting alone.

261 Paragraph 11O provides that, where a devolved authority is making a provision for the purposes of implementing the Protocol, the requirements for consent, joint exercise or consultation with the UK Government will apply where the type of provision would, if made under other powers, require UK Government consent, consultation or joint exercise of powers.

Section 23: Protection for certain rights, safeguards etc. in Belfast Agreement

262 This section is a signpost to Schedule 3, which contains provisions relating to the implementation of Article 2(1) of the Protocol in the Withdrawal Agreement.

Section 24: No alteration of North-South co-operation

263 This section inserts two new subsections into section 10 of the EU (Withdrawal) Act 2018 (entitled 'Continuation of North-South co-operation and the prevention of new border arrangements').

264 New subsection (3) clarifies that a Minister of the Crown may not agree to the making of a recommendation by the Joint Committee under Article 11(2) of the Protocol in relation to recommendations as to North-South co-operation which would have the effect of:

    a.   altering the arrangements of North-South co-operation as provided for by the Belfast (Good Friday) Agreement 1998;

    b.   establishing new implementation bodies; or

    c.   altering the functions of an existing implementation body.

265 New subsection (4) sets out that, for the purposes of this section, the definition of the Belfast (Good Friday) Agreement 1998 is that given by section 98 of the Northern Ireland Act 1998 and the definition of an implementation body is that given by section 55(3) of the Northern Ireland Act 1998.

These Explanatory Notes relate to the European Union (Withdrawal Agreement) Act 2020 (c.1) which received Royal Assent on 23 January 2020

41

Section 25: Retention of saved EU law at end of implementation period

266 During the implementation period certain EU rules and regulations will continue to apply in the UK. For this reason, this section amends the EU (Withdrawal) Act 2018 so that the conversion of EU law into 'retained EU law', and the domestication of historic CJEU case law, will now take place at the end of the implementation period.

267 Subsection (1)(a) amends section 2 of the EU (Withdrawal) Act 2018 so that the preservation of EU-derived domestic legislation takes effect on IP completion day rather than exit day.

268 Subsection (1)(b) removes the definition of EU-derived domestic legislation from section 2 as the term will instead be defined in new section 1B(7) of the EU (Withdrawal) Act 2018.

269 Subsection (1)(c) inserts further words into section 2(3) of the EU (Withdrawal) Act 2018 providing that the preservation of EU-derived legislation is subject to new section 5A, set out at subsection (5) below.

270 Subsection (2) amends the incorporation of direct EU legislation into retained direct EU legislation at section 3 of the EU (Withdrawal) Act 2018.

271 Subsection (2)(a) amends section (3)(1) of the Act so that the incorporation of direct EU legislation takes effect on IP completion day instead of exit day.

272 Subsection (2)(b)(i) amends the reference to exit day in section 3(2)(a) to IP completion day, so that EU regulations, EU decisions and EU tertiary legislation (now known as delegated and implementing acts) are preserved as they have effect immediately before IP completion day.

273 Subsection 2(b)(ii) adds two conditions to the incorporation of EU regulations, EU decisions and EU tertiary legislation, in the form of two insertions to section 3(2)(a):

    a.   The first, at new subsection (ai), states that, to be retained, any EU regulation, EU decision or EU tertiary legislation must have been applicable to and in the UK by virtue of Part 4 of the Withdrawal Agreement, the implementation period. This means that any EU instruments which were not applicable during the implementation period by virtue of Part 4 of the Withdrawal Agreement will not be preserved.

    b.   The second, at new subsection (bi), excludes from the definition of 'direct EU legislation' in section 3 of the EU (Withdrawal) Act 2018, any EU regulation, EU decision or EU Tertiary legislation so far as it has effect or is to have effect by virtue of new sections 7A and 7B. These sections set up a conduit pipe through which provisions of the Withdrawal Agreement (other than Part 4), and the EEA/ EFTA and Swiss Separation Agreements will flow, including any EU regulation, EU decision or EU Tertiary legislation made applicable by the Withdrawal Agreement.

274 Subsections (2)(b)(iii) and (iv) work together to remove a condition on the incorporation of EU regulations, EU decisions and EU tertiary legislation at section 3(2)(a) of the EU (Withdrawal) Act 2018. Specifically, section 3(2)(a)(ii) of that Act is omitted, as EU decisions addressed only to a Member State other than the UK will not be applicable to and in the UK by virtue of Part 4 of the Withdrawal Agreement. Therefore, section 3(2)(ai) will instead prevent such decisions from being retained.

275 Subsection (2)(c) amends section 3(2)(b) of the EU (Withdrawal) Act 2018 which incorporates Annexes to the EEA Agreement.

    a.   (2)(c)(i) amends section 3(2)(b) of the Act so as to save any Annex to the EEA Agreement as it has effect immediately before IP completion day rather than exit day.

These Explanatory Notes relate to the European Union (Withdrawal Agreement) Act 2020 (c.1) which received Royal Assent on 23 January 2020

42

b. (2)(c)(ii) amends section 3(2)(b) of the Act so that the Annexes are only saved insofar as they have been applicable to and in the UK by virtue of the Part 4 of the Withdrawal Agreement, and not to the extent that they continue to flow into the UK via the pipeline established in new section 7A or 7B.

276 Subsection (2)(d) makes the corresponding amendments to section 3(2)(c) of the EU (Withdrawal) Act 2018 with regards to Protocol 1 of the EEA Agreement. It amends that section so as to incorporate the Protocol as it has effect immediately before IP completion day rather than exit day. It also inserts two subsections which:

a. specify that the Protocol is only saved insofar as it has been applicable to and in the UK by virtue of the Part 4 of the Withdrawal Agreement; and

b. ensure that the Protocol is not saved insofar as it is to continue to flow into the UK by virtue of the conduit pipes at new sections 7A and 7B.

277 Subsection (2)(e) amends section 3(3) of the EU (Withdrawal) Act 2018 so as to define what it means for direct EU legislation to be operative immediately before IP completion day rather than exit day.

278 Subsection (2)(f) makes section 3 of the EU (Withdrawal) Act 2018 subject to new section 5A (savings and incorporation: supplementary) as well as to section 5 and Schedule 1.

279 Subsection (3) amends section 4 of the EU (Withdrawal) Act 2018:

a. (3)(a) amends references in section 4(1) so that any remaining EU rights and obligations which do not fall within sections 2 and 3 of the Act are preserved as they had effect immediately before IP completion day rather than exit day.

b. (3)(b)(i) inserts a new subsection (aa) to section 4(2) so as to make an exception to the saving of the remaining rights and obligations where they will continue to flow into domestic law directly by virtue of new sections 7A or 7B, for the purposes of the Agreements.

c. (3)(b)(ii) amends the reference to 'exit day' to 'IP completion day' in section 4(2)(b) of the EU (Withdrawal) Act 2018 so that rights, powers, liabilities, obligations, restrictions, remedies or procedures are not saved under section 4(1) of the Act so far as they arise under an EU Directive and are not recognised by the European Court of Justice or any court or tribunal in the UK in a case decided before IP completion day.

280 Subsection (3)(c) amends section 4 of the EU (Withdrawal) Act 2018 so it is subject to new section 5A (savings and incorporation: supplementary).

281 Subsection (4) amends section 5 of the EU (Withdrawal) Act 2018 on exceptions to savings and incorporation.

282 Subsection (4)(a) amends that section so that the exceptions to the savings and incorporation operate on IP completion day rather than on exit day.

283 Subsection(4)(b) inserts new subsection (7) into section 5 of the EU (Withdrawal) Act 2018. The new subsection ensures that the exceptions to the savings and incorporation set out in section 5 (1) to (6) and in Schedule 1 to that Act, do not apply in relation to relevant separation agreement law as provided for by new section 7C.

These Explanatory Notes relate to the European Union (Withdrawal Agreement) Act 2020 (c.1) which received Royal Assent on 23 January 2020

43

284 Subsection (5) inserts a new section 5A to the EU (Withdrawal) Act 2018. New section 5A is designed to make clear that the law saved and incorporated by sections 2 to 4 of the EU (Withdrawal) Act 2018 continues to have effect on and after IP completion day, despite the fact that the law only applied for the duration of the implementation period under the Withdrawal Agreement.

285 Subsection (6) amends Schedule 1 of the EU (Withdrawal) Act 2018, on further provision about exceptions to savings and incorporation. Subsection (6)(a) amends that Schedule so that the exceptions to the preservation of retained EU law take effect on IP completion day, rather than exit day. Subsection (6)(b) makes sure that references to the principle of the supremacy of EU law, the Charter of Fundamental Rights, any general principle of EU law or the rule in Francovich are to be read as references to that principle, Charter or rule so far as it would otherwise continue to be, or form part of, domestic law on or after IP completion day by virtue of the named provisions of the (amended) EU (Withdrawal) Act 2018.

Section 26: Interpretation of retained EU law and relevant separation agreement law

286 This section defines the term 'relevant separation agreement law' and provides for rules of interpretation in order to ensure that as far as they are applicable, that body of law is interpreted in accordance with the Withdrawal Agreement, the EEA EFTA Separation Agreement and the Swiss Citizens' Rights Agreement. It also allows for a Minister of the Crown, acting after consultation, to provide regulations on how UK courts can interpret retained EU law, including providing for the circumstances under which relevant courts or tribunals are not bound by retained EU case law. The regulations may also set the test that is to be applied in deciding whether to depart from such retained EU case law. The regulations may, however, provide that the test may be determined by a given list of members of the judiciary.

287 Subsection (1) amends section 6 of the EU (Withdrawal) Act 2018 on the interpretation of retained EU law. Specifically:

   a. subsection (1)(a) substitutes references to 'exit day' to 'IP completion day', so that retained EU law, and its accompanying rules of interpretation, come into force on IP completion day;

   b. subsection (1)(b) inserts a new subsection (4)(ba) which provides that a relevant court or relevant tribunal is not bound by any retained EU case law to the extent that this is provided for by regulations made under subsection (5A);

   c. subsection (1)(c) amends subsection (5) to clarify the test that the Supreme Court and High Court of Justiciary must apply when departing from retained EU case law (the same test it must apply when deciding whether to depart from its own case law.

   d. subsection (1)(d) inserts new subsections (5A) to (5D) into section 6).

   e. New subsection (5A) gives a Minister of the Crown the power to make regulations which:

      i.   provide that a court or tribunal is a relevant court or tribunal for the purposes of the section;

      ii. set out the extent to which, or circumstances in which, a relevant court or relevant tribunal is not to be bound by retained EU case law;

      iii. set out the test that the court or tribunal must apply in deciding whether to depart from any retained EU case law; or

iv. provide for considerations which are relevant to the test that the Supreme Court or High Court of Justiciary will apply in accordance with subsection (5) or a relevant court of tribunal apply by virtue of the regulations.

f. New subsection (5B) provides a non-exhaustive list of what the regulations may include:

   i. that the High Court of Justiciary may be a relevant court when sitting for a purpose other than mentioned in subsection (4)(b)(i) and (ii);

   ii. the extent to which, or circumstances in which, a relevant court or tribunal not being bound by retained EU case law includes, or otherwise, that court or tribunal also not being bound by retained domestic case law which relates to retained EU case law;

   iii. other matters arising in relation to retained domestic case law that relates to retained EU case law;

   iv. the test or considerations to be determined by one of the named members of the judiciary under subsection (5C)(a) to (e) (either alone or acting jointly). The regulations may also provide whether that determination is to be made with or without the consent of a Minister of the Crown.

g. New subsection (5C) places an obligation on the Minister when making regulations to consult with a defined list of members of the judiciary, as well as other persons as that Minister considers appropriate;

h. New subsection (5D) provides that the regulations made under subsection (5A) must not be made after IP completion day;

i. Subsection (e) inserts a new subsection 6A into the EU (Withdrawal) Act 2018 which provides that the rules on interpretation of retained EU law in section 6 (1) to (6) of the EU (Withdrawal) Act 2018 are subject to relevant separation agreement law for which the rules of interpretation are set out in new section 7C of the EU (Withdrawal) Act 2018.

288 Subsection (2) inserts a new section 7C after new section 7B of the EU (Withdrawal) Act 2018.

289 New section 7C(1)(a) states that any question concerning the validity, meaning or effect of any relevant separation agreement law is to be decided in accordance with the Withdrawal Agreement, the EEA EFTA Separation Agreement and the Swiss Citizens' Rights Agreement (so far as they are applicable to it). New section 7C(1)(b) provides that regard should be had to the desirability of ensuring that the effect of relevant separation agreement law in relation to matters dealt with by corresponding provisions amongst the Agreements is consistent.

290 New section 7C(2) is a signpost to relevant provisions of each of the Agreements regarding the interpretation of 'relevant separation agreement law'.

291 New section 7C(3) defines 'relevant separation agreement law'. This includes domestic provisions implementing the Agreements and anything which is domestic law by virtue of those provisions (paragraph (a))—either because it flows into domestic law by virtue of the new section 7A and 7B conduit pipes or is made in exercise of the powers listed in new section 7C(3)(a)—and anything else which is domestic law for the purposes of, or otherwise within the scope of the Agreements (subsection (b)), with the exception of Part 4 of the Withdrawal Agreement, which is legislated for separately (that legislation being repealed, in the main, on IP completion day).

These Explanatory Notes relate to the European Union (Withdrawal Agreement) Act 2020 (c.1) which received Royal Assent on 23 January 2020

45

Section 27: Dealing with deficiencies in retained EU law

292 EU law will generally apply in the UK until the end of the implementation period. The Act therefore amends the EU (Withdrawal) Act 2018 so that the conversion of EU law into 'retained EU law', and the domestication of historic CJEU case law, can take place at the end of the implementation period. It also amends the deficiencies power at section 8 of the EU (Withdrawal) Act 2018 so that it will still work in light of the implementation period.

293 This section amends the power at section 8 of the EU (Withdrawal) Act 2018 to extend it so that it can operate on deficiencies that result from the end of the implementation period or any other effect of the withdrawal agreement. It is necessary to do this because the power will need to operate on 'retained EU law' as it stands at the end of the implementation period.

294 Subsection (1) establishes that this section will amend the section 8 power of the EU (Withdrawal) Act 2018.

295 Subsection (2) amends section 8(2) of the EU (Withdrawal) Act 2018 so that the power is available to correct deficiencies arising from withdrawal including the end of the implementation period. This subsection establishes the circumstances in which deficiencies in retained EU law can arise, and therefore which the power provided at section (8)(1) can work upon. This includes:

   a. amendments to section 8(2)(d)(ii) to enable it to deal with deficiencies arising from any arrangements that are dependent upon the UK's membership of the EU or Part 4 of the Withdrawal Agreement and no longer exist or are no longer appropriate;

   b. amendments to section 8(2)(e) to enable it to deal with deficiencies arising from provisions on reciprocal or other arrangements between the UK and other EU Member States that are no longer in place or are no longer appropriate as a result of the UK ceasing to be a party to any of the EU Treaties or as a result of the end of the implementation period or any other effect of the withdrawal agreement;

   c. the inclusion of an additional deficiency which the section 8 power can operate upon, where retained EU law is not clear in its effect as a result of uncertainty from the saving and exceptions to EU law in sections 2 to 6 and Schedule 1 of the EU (Withdrawal) Act 2018, which includes the glosses applied during the implementation period (subsection (2)(c)); and

   d. amendments to section 8(2)(f)(i) of the EU (Withdrawal) Act 2018 so that the deficiencies power can be used where elements of directives have not been implemented into UK domestic law by IP completion day, but it is nonetheless appropriate to retain them.

296 Subsection (3) amends section 8(4) of the EU (Withdrawal) Act 2018 to substitute the reference to 'exit day' to 'IP completion day'. This ensures that retained EU law will not be deficient just because the EU subsequently makes changes to EU law when it no longer applies in the UK by virtue of Part 4 of the Withdrawal Agreement. The subsequent divergence between UK and EU law will not therefore by itself make domestic law deficient.

297 Subsection (4) removes the restriction on the deficiencies power being used to implement the Withdrawal Agreement at section 8(7)(e) of the EU (Withdrawal) Act 2018. For example, this means the power could be re-exercised to revoke deficiencies SIs due to come into force at the end of the implementation period if they would breach provisions of the Withdrawal Agreement that will apply after the end of the implementation period, such as the arrangements on citizens' rights.

These Explanatory Notes relate to the European Union (Withdrawal Agreement) Act 2020 (c.1) which received Royal Assent on 23 January 2020

46

298 Subsection (5) extends the sunset on the deficiencies power at section 8(8) so that it will expire two years after the end of the implementation period rather than two years after exit day. The existing sunset would allow the government limited time following IP completion day to identify and correct deficiencies with this power. It is possible that some deficiencies will only become apparent after the conversion of EU law has taken place and time will be needed to make the necessary legislation to fix them.

299 Subsection (6) clarifies that a deficiency 'arising from the withdrawal of the United Kingdom from the EU' in section 8(1) of the EU (Withdrawal) Act 2018 includes within its definition deficiencies which arise from the end of the implementation period or any other effect of the Withdrawal Agreement.

300 Further, subsection (6) provides that the meaning of deficiency can cover a deficiency that arises out of withdrawal taken together with the operation of, or interaction between, provisions of the EU (Withdrawal) Act 2018 or this Act.

301 Subsection (7) substitutes references to 'exit day' across Part 1 of Schedule 2 of the EU (Withdrawal) Act 2018 to 'IP completion day'. Part 1 of Schedule 2 provides the devolved authorities, and a Minister of the Crown acting jointly with a devolved authority, with power corresponding to the power in section 8 of that Act. The references to 'exit day' in paragraphs 4(a), 8(2)(a)(i), 9(2)(a)(i) and 10(2)(a)(i) of Schedule 2 are amended to 'IP completion day' as a result of the implementation period.

Section 28: Ancillary fee-charging powers

302 Amendments to Schedule 4 of the EU (Withdrawal) Act 2018 allow the fee-charging powers that already exist under that Act to also be used in connection with the Other Separation Issues, and the Protocol on Ireland/Northern Ireland.

303 This allows appropriate authorities that have been given functions under new sections 8B and section 8C (or the corresponding powers for the devolved authorities at new Part 1B and Part 1C of Schedule 2) to make provision in connection with fees or other charges. Regulations made under these powers which do not relate to the altering of a fee or charge to reflect changes in the value of money are subject to the affirmative procedure. Otherwise, the negative procedure applies. The time limit for existing powers in the EU (Withdrawal) Act 2018 does not apply here.

Section 29: Review of EU legislation during implementation period

304 This section will insert a new section 13A into the EU (Withdrawal) Act 2018. It provides additional parliamentary scrutiny for new EU legislation that is made or may be made during the implementation period.

305 Subsection (1) describes the requirements that a report must meet to trigger the procedure in subsection (2). The requirements are that it is the view of the ESC that any EU legislation that is made, or may be made, during the implementation period raises a matter of vital national interest to the UK; that the ESC has taken account of appropriate evidence and consulted departmental select committees; and that the report sets out the wording of a resultant motion to be moved in the House of Commons.

306 Subsection (2) provides that a Minister must make arrangements for a motion to be debated and voted on within 14 sitting days in the House of Commons where a report is published by the European Scrutiny Committee ('ESC') which meets the requirements set out in subsection (1).

These Explanatory Notes relate to the European Union (Withdrawal Agreement) Act 2020 (c.1) which received Royal Assent on 23 January 2020

47

307 Subsection (3) describes the requirements that a report must meet to trigger the procedure in subsection (4), namely that it is the view of the House of Lords EU Select Committee (EUC) that any EU legislation that is made, or may be made, during the implementation period raises a matter of vital national interest to the UK; that the EUC has taken such evidence that it considers appropriate as to the effect of the EU legislation; and that the report sets out the wording of a resultant motion to be moved in the House of Lords.

308 Subsection (4) provides that a Minister of the Crown must make arrangements for a motion to be debated and voted on within 14 sitting days in the House of Lords where a report is published by the House of Lords EU Select Committee (EUC) that meets the requirements set out in subsection (3).

309 Sub-section (5) sets out definitions for terms in this section.

Section 30: Certain dispute procedures under withdrawal agreement

310 This section inserts a new section 13B into the EU (Withdrawal) Act 2018 that requires a Minister of the Crown to provide Parliament with a written statement where, after the IP, certain formal dispute procedures are used between the UK and EU.

311 Title III of Part 6 of the Withdrawal Agreement provides for a dispute resolution mechanism for most disputes that arise between the UK and the EU after the end of the implementation period. It provides that the UK and the EU must endeavour to resolve disputes by entering into consultation in the Joint Committee. If this is not possible, the dispute may be referred to an independent arbitration panel, comprised of suitable arbitrators. If a dispute submitted to the panel requires an interpretation of EU law (or raises a question of the UK's compliance with certain obligations), Article 174 of the Withdrawal Agreement requires the panel to request a ruling from the CJEU on the issue.

312 New section 13B requires a Minister of the Crown to inform Parliament of various steps taken in connection with a dispute between the EU and the UK about the interpretation and application of the Withdrawal Agreement.

313 Subsections (1) and (2) provide that where a request is made to the other party to establish an arbitration panel under Article 170 a Minister must within 14 days make a written statement to Parliament setting out the request and the details.

314 Subsections (3) and (4) provide that where the CJEU has given a ruling in response to a request by an arbitration panel under Article 174(1) of the withdrawal agreement, a Minister must within 14 days of the ruling being published in the Official Journal, make a written statement to Parliament setting out details.

315 Subsection (5) provides a Minister must, after the end of each reporting period, lay a report before Parliament detailing the number of times within a reporting period that the Joint Committee has been provided with notice under Article 169(1) to commence consultations to resolve a dispute between the EU and UK on the interpretation and/or application of the Withdrawal Agreement.

316 Subsection (6) defines 'reporting period' and the '14 day period'.

These Explanatory Notes relate to the European Union (Withdrawal Agreement) Act 2020 (c.1) which received Royal Assent on 23 January 2020

48

Section 31: Repeal of section 13 of the EU (Withdrawal) Act 2018

317 Section 13 of the EU (Withdrawal) Act 2018 sets out the process for 'Parliamentary approval of the outcome of negotiations with the EU'. It provides that the Withdrawal Agreement may only be ratified if the House of Commons has approved, by resolution, the negotiated Withdrawal Agreement and the framework for the future relationship, a take note motion has been tabled in the House of Lords, so that both documents can be debated, and an Act of Parliament has been passed which contains provision implementing the Agreement.

318 Subsection (1) of section 31 repeals section 13 of the EU (Withdrawal) Act 2018, to ensure that the Withdrawal Agreement can be ratified in a timely and orderly manner, and to remove provisions that are no longer needed.

319 Further, subsection (2) clarifies that the specific conditions set out in section 13(1)(a) to (d) therefore do not apply before ratification of the Withdrawal Agreement. While the condition in section 1(d) is removed, the Act still implements the Withdrawal Agreement, as is required for the Withdrawal Agreement to have domestic legal effect. The Act is also required before the UK Government can ratify the Withdrawal Agreement and then leave the EU.

Section 32: Requirements in Part 2 of CRAGA

320 Section 20 of the Constitutional Reform and Governance Act 2010 sets out certain conditions that must be met before treaties can be ratified. These are that: a Minister of the Crown has laid before Parliament a copy of the treaty, the treaty has been published, and the relevant period (21 sitting days) has passed without either House having resolved that the treaty should not be ratified.

321 Section 32 disapplies section 20 of the Constitutional Reform and Governance Act 2010 in relation to the Withdrawal Agreement. This enables ratification of the Withdrawal Agreement to take place without the conditions of section 20 having been met, and avoids any additional delay that could be created by the 21 day process. The provision does not extend to future modifications of the Withdrawal Agreement agreed by the Joint Committee, to which section 20 may apply.

Section 33: Prohibition on extending the implementation period

322 This section prevents the extension of the implementation period. It does so by prohibiting a Minister of the Crown agreeing to an extension in the Joint Committee. This is a domestic law measure; Article 132 of the Withdrawal Agreement is unchanged.

Section 34: Ministerial co-chairs of the Joint Committee

323 This provision requires the functions of the co-chair of the Joint Committee established under Article 164 of the Withdrawal Agreement and as described in Annex VIII to the Withdrawal Agreement (Rules of procedure of the Joint Committee and Specialised Committee) to be exercised personally by a Government Minister. Further, it expressly clarifies that only a Minister of the Crown may attend meetings as a replacement for the UK representative co-chair under Rule 1.3 of the Rules of Procedure.

324 The aim of this provision is to ensure that there is ministerial oversight of the Joint Committee and the effect of the provision is that co-chair functions may not be delegated to officials.

These Explanatory Notes relate to the European Union (Withdrawal Agreement) Act 2020 (c.1) which received Royal Assent on 23 January 2020

49

Section 35: No use of written procedure in the Joint Committee

325 The provision precludes a Minister of the Crown, as the UK's co-chair, using the written procedure (Annex VIII, Rule 9 of the Withdrawal Agreement) to adopt recommendations or decisions of the Joint Committee. This ensures that decisions made by the Joint Committee are made by a Minister in person. The purpose of this provision is to ensure there is full ministerial accountability, including to Parliament, for all decisions made in the Joint Committee.

Section 36: Repeal of unnecessary or spent enactments

326 Section 36 provides for the repeal of unnecessary or spent enactments passed in the previous Parliament in relation to the UK's exit from the EU.

327 Subsection (a) repeals section 9 of EU (Withdrawal) Act 2018 which gives Ministers of the Crown a power to make secondary legislation to implement the withdrawal agreement agreed between the UK and the EU under Article 50(2) of the TEU. This power, which expires on exit day, is redundant and no longer necessary in light of this Act which will implement the withdrawal agreement.

328 Subsection (b) repeals the duties under sections 16 and 18 of EU (Withdrawal) Act 2018 which have been fulfilled. Section 16 required the Secretary of State to publish draft legislation (and a policy statement) containing requirements relating to environmental principles within 6 months of the EU (Withdrawal) Act 2018 receiving Royal Assent. The draft Environment (Principles and Governance) Act 2018 and statement of policy was published in December 2018. Section 18 required a Minister of the Crown to lay before each House of Parliament a written statement outlining the steps taken by the Government, in negotiations to withdraw from the EU, to seek to negotiate an agreement to participate in a customs arrangement as part of the framework for the UK's future relationship with the EU before the end of 31 October 2018. This statement was published on 25 October 2018. As these duties have been fulfilled these provisions are now redundant and are therefore being repealed.

329 Subsection (c) repeals section 19 of the EU (Withdrawal) Act 2018. This section makes clear that nothing in that Act prevents the UK from replicating EU law in domestic law made on or after exit day, or from continuing to participate in, or have a formal relationship with, agencies of the EU after exit day. However, this provision has no legal effect in practice and is therefore unnecessary so is being repealed.

330 Subsection (d) repeals Part 2 of Schedule 2 to the EU (Withdrawal) Act 2018, which provides a corresponding power to section 9 given to the devolved authorities to implement the withdrawal agreement. It is being repealed for the same reason as the repeal of section 9.

331 Subsection (e) repeals the European Union (Withdrawal) Act 2019 which required the Government to request an extension of the period in Article 50(3) of the TEU and seek parliamentary approval for the agreed extension date. The principal duties in connection with the Article 50 extension have been spent and no longer have any legal effect so are being repealed. Paragraph 65 of Schedule 5 to this Act saves the amendment which was made by section 2 of this Act to the procedure for section 20(4) of the EU (Withdrawal) Act 2018 to make regulations amending the definition of exit day.

These Explanatory Notes relate to the European Union (Withdrawal Agreement) Act 2020 (c.1) which received Royal Assent on 23 January 2020

50

332 Subsection (f) repeals the European Union (Withdrawal) (No. 2) Act 2019 which required the Prime Minister to seek an extension of the period under Article 50(3) TEU by 19 October 2019 in certain circumstances. It also placed requirements on the Government to report on the progress of negotiations on the UK's relationship with the EU. The principal duty in the Act of seeking an extension by 19 October 2019 has been fulfilled and no longer has any legal effect so is being repealed. The remaining reporting and parliamentary debate obligations are also being repealed as these are no longer necessary. Paragraph 65 of Schedule 5 to this Act saves the amendment which was made by section 4 of this Act to section 20(4) of the EU (Withdrawal) Act 2018, which provides for regulations to be made amending the definition of exit day.

Section 37: Arrangements with the EU about unaccompanied children seeking asylum

333 Section 17 of the EU (Withdrawal) Act 2018 sets out a negotiating requirement for a Minister of the Crown to seek an agreement with the EU to ensure that an unaccompanied child who has made a claim for international protection in a Member State can come to the UK to join a relative, and that an unaccompanied child in the UK can join a relative in the EU in equivalent circumstances.

334 Section 37 amends subsection (1) of section 17 of the EU (Withdrawal) Act 2018 to remove the obligation to seek to negotiate such an agreement and replace it with a requirement to make a statement to Parliament.

335 The requirement obliges a Minister of the Crown to make a single statement to Parliament within two months of Royal Assent setting out the Government's policy intentions in respect of any future arrangements with the EU in relation to family reunification for unaccompanied children seeking international protection in the UK or EU.

Section 38: Parliamentary sovereignty

336 Section 38 addresses the relationship between the constitutional principle of Parliamentary sovereignty and the law made applicable by the separation agreements as it would apply in the UK after exit day by virtue of the Withdrawal Agreement, EEA EFTA Separation Agreement and Swiss Citizens' Rights Agreement. The section recognises that the application of this law through the Withdrawal Agreement Act does not constitute a derogation from the principle of Parliamentary sovereignty.

337 Subsection (1) recognises that, as a matter of common law, the Parliament of the United Kingdom is sovereign.

338 As above, sections 1, 5, 6, and 26 provide for the direct application of the separation agreements in domestic law. Subsection (2) recognises that the principle of Parliamentary sovereignty subsists despite the effect of these sections.

339 Subsection (3) recognises that, accordingly, nothing in the Withdrawal Agreement Act derogates from the fundamental principle of Parliamentary sovereignty. This proposition flows from the observations established in subsections (1) and (2).

340 As such, the section acknowledges the pre-existing legal position as regards Parliamentary sovereignty.

Section 39: Interpretation

341 Subsection (1) defines certain terms used throughout the Act.

These Explanatory Notes relate to the European Union (Withdrawal Agreement) Act 2020 (c.1) which received Royal Assent on 23 January 2020

51

342 Subsection (2) makes further provision about the meaning of references to IP completion day. References to before, after or on IP completion day or to beginning with IP completion day are to be read as references to before, after or at 11.00 p.m. on 31 December 2020 or (as the case may be) to beginning with 11.00 p.m. on that day.

343 Subsections (3) to (5) deal with changes to IP completion day. Subsection (3) sets out when the power at subsection (4) to amend the definition of IP completion day may be used. The power may only be used to take account of any changes to EU summertime arrangements. Subsection (4) then provides for the power to be exercised by a Minister of the Crown, with subsection (5) defining what is meant by the term 'EU summertime arrangements' in this section.

344 Subsection (6) clarifies that references to Articles of the Treaty on European Union also include references to those Articles as applied by the Euratom Treaty.

Section 40: Regulations

345 This section provides that Schedule 4 of the Act contains provisions about regulations in the Act. This includes provision about the parliamentary procedures applicable to the exercise of the powers in the Act.

Section 41: Consequential and transitional provisions

346 Subsection (1) allows a Minister of the Crown to make regulations which are appropriate as a consequence of the Act.

347 Subsection (2) clarifies that consequential provision might include modifying (such as amending, repealing or revoking) both primary and secondary legislation.

348 Subsection (3) provides that Ministers cannot make consequential provision which modifies primary legislation (which includes secondary legislation made under that primary legislation) passed after IP completion day.

349 Subsection (4) provides that Parts 1 and 2 of Schedule 5 contains minor and consequential provision.

350 Subsection (5) allows a Minister of the Crown to make transitional, transitory or saving provision by regulations.

351 Subsection (6) provides that Part 3 of Schedule 5 contains transitional, transitory and saving provision.

Section 42: Extent, commencement and short title

352 Subsection (1) provides that the Act extends to the legal jurisdictions of England and Wales, Scotland and Northern Ireland, subject to subsections (2) to (5).

353 Subsection (2) provides that any provision of the Act which amends or repeals an enactment has the same extent as the enactment it is amending or repealing.

354 Subsection (3) makes it clear that section 1 (the saving of the ECA for the implementation period) extends to the Isle of Man, the Channel Islands and Gibraltar.

355 Subsection (4) provides that the power in section 36 of the Immigration Act 1971 and section 60(4) of the UK Borders Act 2007 may be exercised to extend to the Channel Islands or Isle of Man the modifications to those Acts made by section 10.

356 Subsection (5) provides that paragraphs 1 and 2 of Schedule 5 so far as they relate to the modification of subordinate legislation which extends outside England and Wales, Scotland and Northern Ireland, also extend there.

These Explanatory Notes relate to the European Union (Withdrawal Agreement) Act 2020 (c.1) which received Royal Assent on 23 January 2020

52

357 Subsection (6) specifies which provisions come into force on Royal Assent.

358 Subsection (7) sets out that the remaining provisions will come into force on the day or days appointed by regulations, and different days may be appointed for different purposes.

359 Subsection (8) establishes that the short title of the Act is the European Union (Withdrawal Agreement) Act 2020.

Schedule 1: Powers of devolved authorities under sections 12, 13 and 14

No power to make provision outside devolved competence

360 Paragraph 1 provides that the powers in respect of social security co-ordination, recognition of professional qualifications and equal treatment under sections 12, 13 or 14 cannot be used outside of devolved competence, where exercised by devolved authorities acting alone. This maintains the status quo in respect of the competence of the devolved authorities and ability to act in these areas.

361 Paragraph 2 relates to the competence of Scottish Ministers. Sub-paragraph (a) relates to legislative competence and sets out that the Scottish Ministers may exercise these powers where the Scottish Parliament has legislative competence. The definition of 'legislative competence' for the purposes of exercising these powers disapplies the normal restriction on the Scottish Parliament's competence, which prevents the Scottish Parliament from legislating in a way that is incompatible with EU law. This disapplication is necessary to enable the Scottish Ministers to make all necessary regulations under these powers in devolved areas.

362 Sub-paragraph (b) relates to those secondary legislation-making powers which are not within legislative competence but are within the executive competence of the Scottish Ministers. The definition of 'executive competence' for the purposes of exercising these powers disapplies the normal restriction on the Scottish Ministers' competence which prevents the Scottish Ministers from legislating in a way that is incompatible with EU law. The restrictions relating to retained EU law are also disapplied for the purposes of defining legislative and executive competence.

363 Paragraph 3 relates to the competence of the Welsh Ministers and makes the same provision for the Welsh Ministers as for the Scottish Ministers as set out in paragraph 2. The Welsh Ministers will be able to exercise these powers in areas within the National Assembly for Wales' legislative competence (disapplying the restrictions preventing the National Assembly for Wales from legislating in a way that is incompatible with EU law or from modifying retained EU law) and to amend legislation which has been made under their executive competence.

364 Paragraph 4 relates to the competence of Northern Ireland departments. Sub-paragraph (a) deals with transferred matters, providing that Northern Ireland devolved authorities may make regulations using the power in any areas which would be within the Northern Ireland Assembly's legislative competence and which would not require consent of the Secretary of State for Northern Ireland. Sub-paragraph (b) deals with reserved matters, providing that where Northern Ireland legislation has previously been made in relation to reserved matters, Northern Ireland departments and Ministers will be able to use the power to amend this legislation. In both sub-paragraphs (a) and (b) the existing restrictions on legislative competence that would make it outside of legislative competence to act in a way that is incompatible with EU law, or to modify retained EU law, are disapplied in defining legislative competence for the purpose of these powers. Sub-paragraph (c) makes the same provision as for Scottish and Welsh Ministers so that Northern Ireland departments can exercise the power to amend legislation which has been made under their executive competence.

These Explanatory Notes relate to the European Union (Withdrawal Agreement) Act 2020 (c.1) which received Royal Assent on 23 January 2020

53

Requirement for consent where it would otherwise be required

365 Paragraph 5 sets out that if a devolved authority is making a provision using these powers that would require consent if it were a provision in legislation of the relevant devolved legislature or where the devolved administration would normally require consent to make such a provision via secondary legislation, then that consent will still be required. This will not apply if the devolved authority already has power to make such provision using secondary legislation without needing the consent of the Minister of the Crown.

Requirement for joint exercise where it would otherwise be required

366 Paragraph 6 sets out that where a devolved authority would normally only be able to make legislation jointly with the UK Government, the devolved authority will still have to make such legislation jointly when exercising the power.

Requirement for consultation where it would otherwise be required

367 Paragraph 7 requires consultation with the UK Government on legislation made by a devolved authority in the exercise of the power, where the devolved authority would normally be required to consult with the UK Government when making those kind of changes in legislation.

Interpretation

368 Paragraph 8 defines a Northern Ireland devolved authority as the First Minister and deputy First Minister in Northern Ireland acting jointly, a Northern Ireland Minister, or a Northern Ireland department.

Schedule 2: Independent Monitoring Authority for the Citizens' Rights Agreements

Part 1: Constitution, proceedings etc

Status

369 Paragraph 1 sets out that the IMA is not to be a Crown body.

Membership

370 Paragraph 2 sets out the membership of the IMA (effectively its decision-making board). Sub-paragraph (1) lists this membership as a chair (a non-executive), a chief executive officer (an executive, who will be an employee of the IMA), and at least two but no more than six other non-executive members and at least one but no more than three other executive members. The Secretary of State is to appoint the non-executive members. The Secretary of State and the non-executive members must ensure, so far as is practicable, that the number of non-executive members exceeds the number of executive members, in order to ensure effective oversight. Sub-paragraph (7) provides that a member may not be a civil servant. Once the chair and at least two other non-executive members have been appointed, all of the appointed non-executive members are to appoint the executive members, who shall be employees of the IMA, but must consult the Secretary of State on the appointment of the chief executive officer.

Interim chief executive

371 Paragraph 3 allows the Secretary of State to appoint a chief executive for an interim period prior to a chief executive being appointed in accordance with paragraph 2(3). Before the membership of the IMA is fully constituted in accordance with paragraph 2(1), the chief executive appointed by the Secretary of State may undertake matters on behalf of the IMA including incurring expenditure, subject to any directions given by the Secretary of State.

These Explanatory Notes relate to the European Union (Withdrawal Agreement) Act 2020 (c.1) which received Royal Assent on 23 January 2020

54

372 Paragraph 4 defines the desired expertise to be held collectively by the IMA's members. When making appointments, the Secretary of State and the non-executive members must have regard to the desirability of IMA members having knowledge of conditions in the UK relating to matters in Part 2 of the Withdrawal Agreement (for example social security co-ordination, or the recognition of professional qualifications) and the equivalent Part in the EEA EFTA Separation Agreement, referred to as 'relevant matters.'

373 Sub-paragraph (2) sets out that the Secretary of State must ensure, as far as is possible, that the IMA membership includes non-executive members with knowledge of the conditions in Scotland, Wales and Northern Ireland respectively, in relation to Part 2 of the Withdrawal Agreement and EEA EFTA Separation Agreement. This is to reflect the fact that the IMA will exercise its functions across all areas of the UK.

374 Sub-paragraph (3) provides that where the IMA exercises functions in relation to Gibraltar, the Secretary of State must ensure, so far as possible, that there is a non-executive member who knows about conditions in Gibraltar in relation to Part 2 of the Withdrawal Agreement and Part 2 of the EEA EFTA Separation Agreement.

375 Sub-paragraph (4) and (5) requires the Secretary of State or non-executive members to be satisfied that a person does not have a conflict of interest before appointing them. Conflict of interest is defined in sub-paragraph (5) as a person having a financial or other interest which is likely to prejudice their function as a member of the IMA, which might be, for example, a member who sits on another public body that has an interest in the IMA's work.

Procedure for appointing members with knowledge of conditions in devolved areas etc

376 Paragraph 5 sets out the procedures for appointing the non-executive members under paragraph 4(2) and (3). Sub-paragraph (2) requires the Secretary of State to tell the relevant authority (that is, the relevant devolved administration or Gibraltar Minister specified in sub-paragraph (8)) who they propose to appoint and why.

377 Sub-paragraph (3) states that the Secretary of State must appoint that person if the relevant authority agrees to that appointment within a period of one month from the action set out under sub-paragraph (2), subject to sub-paragraph (4).

378 Sub-paragraph (4) states that if the person is no longer available, or if the Secretary of State and the relevant authority agree that the person should not be appointed following the process set out in sub-paragraph (3) (for example, due to new circumstances that indicate that the appointment may no longer be appropriate), then the Secretary of State must propose to appoint a different person following the process set out in sub-paragraph (2) and (3) again.

379 Sub-paragraph (5) sets out the process following sub-paragraph (3), in the event that the relevant authority does not agree to the Secretary of State's proposed appointee. The Secretary of State may either make the appointment without the agreement of the relevant authority (sub-paragraph (5)(a)) or the Secretary of State may propose to appoint a different person (sub-paragraph (5)(b)).

380 Sub-paragraph (6) states that the process set out in sub-paragraphs (2) to (5) is repeated if the Secretary of State proposes to appoint a different person under sub-paragraph (5)(b).

381 Sub-paragraph (7) states that the Secretary of State must publish a written statement explaining the decision to proceed with a proposed appointment without the agreement of the relevant authority under sub-paragraph (5)(a).

382 Sub-paragraph (8) defines a relevant authority for the purposes of sub-paragraphs (1) to (7).

These Explanatory Notes relate to the European Union (Withdrawal Agreement) Act 2020 (c.1) which received Royal Assent on 23 January 2020

55

Non-executive members: terms of appointment and tenure etc

383 Paragraph 6 provides that a person holds and vacates office as a member of the IMA in accordance with the terms and conditions of the person's appointment. Terms and conditions will be set out in the person's appointment letter, unless provided for in legislation.

384 Sub-paragraph (2) requires the Secretary of State to set the terms and conditions for non-executive appointments, subject to the provisions contained in the Schedule.

385 Sub-paragraphs (3) and (4) set the term limits for board members of the IMA. The chair will be appointed for a period of up to five years with any other non-executive member to be appointed for up to four years.

386 Sub-paragraph (5) provides that non-executive members may resign by giving written notice to the Secretary of State.

387 Sub-paragraph (6) gives the Secretary of State the power to remove a non-executive member of the IMA on the grounds specified in sub-paragraph (7). Before doing so, the Secretary of State is under a duty to consult the other non-executive members.

388 Sub-paragraph (7) sets out the grounds upon which non-executive members of the IMA may be removed from office under sub-paragraph (6). These are:

  a. absence from meetings for a continuous period of more than six months without the IMA's permission;

  b. if the member has a conflict of interest preventing the member from carrying out the functions of the office;

  c. if the member has been convicted of a criminal offence;

  d. if the Secretary of State is of the opinion that the member is unable, unwilling or unfit to carry out the functions of the office; and

  e. on any other grounds set out in the member's terms of appointment.

Remuneration of non-executive members

389 Paragraph 7 provides for the Secretary of State to determine the remuneration, allowances and gratuities to be paid to non-executive members of the IMA. Sub-paragraphs (3) and (4) provide that the IMA must make a payment to a non-executive member as the Secretary of State may determine where the term of the non-executive member has not expired, they cease to hold office, and the Secretary of State thinks there are special circumstances that make it right for that member to receive compensation.

Staffing of the IMA

390 Paragraph 8 sets out that the IMA may appoint employees and arrange for its staffing. Terms and conditions of employment, remuneration and paying of pensions, allowance and gratuities are to be determined by the IMA with the approval of the Secretary of State (except for in the case of a chief executive appointed by the Secretary of State, where these determinations are made by the Secretary of State), as set out in (2) to (4). Sub-paragraph (4) sets out that the IMA must pay or make provisions for payments of pensions, allowances and gratuities to be made, as agreed and approved by the Secretary of State (or, in the case of a chief executive appointed by the Secretary of State, as determined by the Secretary of State). Sub-paragraphs (5) and (6) ensure that the IMA is able to take part in superannuation schemes for its employees.

These Explanatory Notes relate to the European Union (Withdrawal Agreement) Act 2020 (c.1) which received Royal Assent on 23 January 2020

56

391 Sub-paragraph (7) provides that the terms and conditions, remuneration and payment of allowances and expenses under sub-paragraphs (2) to (4) in relation to executive members of the IMA are to be determined by the non-executive members with the approval of the Secretary of State.

Procedure

392 The IMA, as an independent authority, is permitted by paragraph 9 to determine its own procedures and decide how it will operate. This is subject to a number of conditions set out in this paragraph. These conditions are;

    a.   the establishment and maintenance of a register of members' interests;

    b.   the publication of entries recorded in the register; and

    c.   the quorum for a meeting of the IMA being half the number of the members appointed for the time being, with the majority of those present being non-executive members.

393 Sub-paragraph (5) provides that the IMA must establish procedures for dealing with conflicts of interests of its members.

394 Sub-paragraph (6) states that the aforementioned arrangements must oblige each member to declare all financial interests and personal interests relevant to exercise of an IMA function and to withdraw from the exercise of an affected function unless the IMA is satisfied that the interest will not affect its exercise. Sub-paragraph (7) states that the validity of any proceedings of the IMA or of its committees or subcommittees is not affected by any vacancy or defective appointment.

Discharge of functions

395 Paragraph 10 sets out who is permitted to exercise the functions of the IMA. The IMA can authorise its employees, members or committees to do anything the IMA may do, apart from approving an annual report as set out in paragraph 31 (which is a function reserved to the IMA's board). A committee of the IMA under sub-paragraph (2) can authorise a sub-committee, a committee member, a member of the IMA or an employee of the IMA to exercise a function the relevant committee is authorised to carry out. This ability to delegate is intended to ensure operational effectiveness.

396 Sub-paragraph (3) provides that a committee and a sub-committee may include IMA employees who are not members of it.

Seal and evidence

397 Paragraph 11 sets out how the IMA's seal is to be authenticated, and how it should be treated once authenticated. This provision is needed to clarify how documents produced by the IMA can be verified as being official communications, and how these documents should be treated.

398 The IMA's seal is authenticated through the signature of the chief executive of the IMA or another person authorised by the IMA for that purpose. Any document that purports to be executed under the IMA's seal or signed on its behalf is to be received in evidence and taken to be so unless the contrary is shown.

399 Sub-paragraph (3) provides that paragraph 11 does not apply in relation to any document signed in accordance with the law of Scotland.

These Explanatory Notes relate to the European Union (Withdrawal Agreement) Act 2020 (c.1) which received Royal Assent on 23 January 2020

57

Funding

400 Paragraph 12 provides that the Secretary of State must make such payments to the IMA as they consider appropriate for the IMA to be able to perform its functions. This is the mechanism through which the IMA receives its annual budget and means its budget will be supplied by the relevant Government department and accounted for to Parliament as part of that department's spending.

Operational Independence

401 Paragraph 13 provides that, when exercising their functions in respect of the IMA, the Secretary of State must have regard to the need to protect the IMA's operational independence and ability to make impartial assessments.

Accounts and audit

402 Paragraph 14 provides that the IMA must keep proper accounts and records and must prepare a statement of accounts for each financial year. It must comply with directions from the Secretary of State on how the statement of accounts should be prepared.

403 Sub-paragraph (3) places a duty on the IMA to send a copy of each statement of accounts to the Secretary of State and the Comptroller and Auditor General by the end of August next following the financial year to which the statement relates.

404 Sub-paragraph (4) sets out the duties of the Comptroller and Auditor General in relation to these accounts, which are to examine, certify, and report on each annual statement of accounts. They must also lay a copy of the statement and the report on the statement before Parliament within four months from when the Comptroller and Auditor General receives the statement.

405 Sub-paragraph (5) defines the term 'financial year' for the purposes of the Schedule as commencing on the day the membership of the IMA is first constituted (in accordance with paragraph 2(1)) and ending on the next 31 March after that day if that results in the first financial year being a period of six months or more; or, otherwise, the second 31 March and each successive period of 12 months thereafter.

Annual plan

406 Paragraph 15 places a duty on the IMA to prepare an annual plan for each financial year on how it intends to perform its functions, with the flexibility to revise the plan. The IMA must submit the annual plan or any revision to the Secretary of State.

407 Sub-paragraph (3) provides that the first annual plan must be submitted within three months from the date the membership of the IMA is first constituted (in accordance with paragraph 2(1)). The plan must relate to the remainder of the financial year in which the IMA is established.

408 Sub-paragraph (4) obliges the IMA to submit subsequent annual plans no later than one month before the beginning of the financial year to which the annual plan relates.

Public records

409 Paragraph 16 ensures that the administrative records of the IMA will be public records.

Investigation by the Parliamentary Commissioner

410 Paragraph 17 ensures that the IMA will be subject to investigation by the Parliamentary Commissioner (the Parliamentary Ombudsman).

These Explanatory Notes relate to the European Union (Withdrawal Agreement) Act 2020 (c.1) which received Royal Assent on 23 January 2020

58

House of Commons disqualification

411 Paragraph 18 ensures that members of the IMA are disqualified from membership of the House of Commons.

Northern Ireland Assembly disqualification

412 Paragraph 19 ensures that members of the IMA are disqualified from membership of the Northern Ireland Assembly. Similar provision will be made in relation to the Scottish Parliament and the Welsh Assembly via the appropriate secondary legislation, in line with the relevant provisions of the Scotland Act 1998 and Government of Wales Act 2006.

Freedom of information

413 Paragraph 20 ensures that the IMA will be subject to the Freedom of Information Act.

Public sector equality duty

414 Paragraph 21 ensures that the IMA will be subject to the public sector equality duty under the Equality Act 2010. Similar provision will be made in relation to Northern Ireland via the appropriate secondary legislation, in line with the relevant provisions of the Northern Ireland Act 1998.

Part 2: Functions of the IMA

General duties

415 Paragraph 22 places a duty on the IMA to monitor the implementation and application of Part 2 of the Withdrawal Agreement and Part 2 of the EEA EFTA Separation Agreement by the UK.

416 Sub-paragraph (2) outlines that the duty includes keeping under review the adequacy and effectiveness of the legislative framework which implements or otherwise deals with matters arising out of or relating to Part 2 and the exercise of functions by public authorities in relation to the same.

417 Sub-paragraph (3) defines 'Part 2' as Part 2 of the Withdrawal Agreement or Part 2 of the EEA EFTA Separation Agreement (the citizens' rights parts of these). The term 'relevant public authority' is taken to include the Secretary of State or any other person who exercises functions of a public nature, but for the exceptions in sub-paragraph (3)(a), (b) and (c).

418 Sub-paragraph (3) provides that the following are not to be regarded as public authorities for the purposes of the IMA: (a) a court or tribunal; (b) either House of Parliament or a person who exercises functions in connection to proceedings in Parliament and; (c) the devolved legislatures or a person who exercises functions in connection to proceedings in the devolved legislatures.

419 Paragraph 23 provides that the IMA must promote the adequate and effective implementation of Part 2 of the Withdrawal Agreement and EEA EFTA Separation Agreement. This could be done, for example, by the IMA exercising its functions in order to identify any potential breaches of Part 2 in the UK and bringing these to the attention of relevant parties. Paragraph 27, for example, obliges the IMA to publish any reports it produces subsequent to an inquiry, as soon as is practicable.

420 Paragraph 24 provides that the IMA must have regard to the importance of addressing general or systemic failings in the implementation or application of Part 2.

These Explanatory Notes relate to the European Union (Withdrawal Agreement) Act 2020 (c.1) which received Royal Assent on 23 January 2020

59

421 Paragraph 25 gives the IMA the power, but not the obligation, to carry out inquiries: in response to a request from a Secretary of State; in response to a request from a Scottish Minister when the request relates to a public authority that is devolved to Scotland; in response to a request from a Welsh Minister when the request relates to an inquiry that is devolved to Wales; in response to a request from the Executive Office in Northern Ireland when the request relates to a public authority that is devolved to Northern Ireland; following a complaint from a person under paragraph 29; or on its own initiative.

422 Sub-paragraph (2) defines that the purposes of an inquiry are for the IMA to determine whether the UK has failed to comply with Part 2 or a relevant public authority has acted or is proposing to act in a way that prevents or would prevent a person from exercising a relevant right. The IMA will identify any recommendations it considers appropriate to be made to a relevant public authority to promote the adequate and effective implementation of Part 2.

423 Sub-paragraph (3) prohibits the IMA from carrying out an inquiry other than one in response to a request from a Secretary of State (or a Scottish Minister, a Welsh Minister, or the Executive Office in Northern Ireland where the inquiry relates to a public authority that is devolved to their respective nations, as set out in paragraph 25), unless there are reasonable grounds to believe that the inquiry in question may conclude that the UK has failed to comply with Part 2, or that a relevant public authority has acted or is proposing to act in a way that prevents a person exercising a relevant right.

424 Sub-paragraphs (4) and (5) give the IMA a discretion not to carry out an inquiry even if the conditions set-out in sub-paragraph (3) are satisfied. This discretion includes where the IMA considers there are no reasonable grounds to believe that an inquiry may identify general or systemic failures in the application of Part 2.

425 Paragraph 26 places a duty on the IMA to publish its intention to carry out an inquiry by any means which it considers appropriate.

426 Sub-paragraph (2) provides that where an inquiry is about matters raised by a person who has made a complaint regarding a relevant right as defined in paragraph 29(1)(a) or (b), the IMA must invite representations from the complainant, any relevant public authority about which the person is complaining and any other person the IMA considers appropriate (for example a relevant regulatory body).

427 Sub-paragraph (3) sets out that in relation to inquiries not prompted by complaints, the IMA must invite representations from any person it considers appropriate. Sub-paragraph (4) requires the IMA to publish how and when people can make representations relating to an inquiry and (5) sets out that the IMA should consider any representations made to it in accordance with sub-paragraph (4) concerning any inquiry.

Reports following an inquiry

428 Paragraph 27 requires the IMA to prepare a written report, including its conclusions and any recommendations to be made to a relevant public authority to promote the adequate and effective implementation or application of Part 2 following the conclusion of an inquiry. A report following an inquiry must then be published as soon as is reasonably practicable after preparing it.

These Explanatory Notes relate to the European Union (Withdrawal Agreement) Act 2020 (c.1) which received Royal Assent on 23 January 2020

60

429 Sub-paragraph (3) places a duty on the IMA to give the Secretary of State an opportunity to require the IMA to remove from a report any material relating to border security or terrorism (including individual cases) that in the Secretary of State's opinion should not be published on the grounds that its publication would be undesirable for reasons of national security or might jeopardise a person's safety. For example, it may be necessary to remove information that could compromise or expose an ongoing counter-terrorism investigation.

430 Sub-paragraph (4) sets out when an IMA report should be published and to whom it should be sent. A report should be published as soon as is reasonably practicable and must then be sent to:

    a.   the Secretary of State, the Scottish Ministers, the Welsh Ministers, and the Executive Office of Northern Ireland;

    b.   any relevant public authority which was invited to make representations in relation to the inquiry;

    c.   any relevant public authority of which a recommendation is made in the report; and

    d.   any other relevant public authority the IMA considers appropriate (for example if they have similar responsibilities).

431 Paragraph 28 provides that where a report includes recommendations to a relevant public authority, the authority must have regard to the recommendations and publish a response expeditiously and in any event within three months beginning with the day on which the IMA published its report. The public authority must explain what it proposes to do in relation to each recommendation, giving reasons, including if it intends to take no action (for example because an issue identified has already been addressed).

Complaints

432 Paragraph 29 allows a person who claims to have relevant right to complain to the IMA where they believe the UK has failed to comply with Part 2 or a relevant public authority has acted or is intending to act in a way that prevents the person from exercising a relevant right.

433 Sub-paragraph (2) requires the IMA to carry out a preliminary review of each complaint to decide whether to carry out an inquiry in relation to it. That decision should be informed by sub-paragraph (3) among other relevant considerations.

434 Sub-paragraph (3) places a duty on the IMA to consider whether it would be more appropriate to resolve a complaint through alternative means before initiating an inquiry. For example, an individual's complaint may already be the subject of legal action or amenable to administrative review.

435 Sub-paragraph (4) provides that the IMA must inform the relevant person if it decides not to carry out an inquiry. The IMA can advise the relevant person on the alternative ways the matters raised in the complaint can be addressed.

Applying for review or intervening in legal proceedings

436 Paragraph 30 gives the IMA the legal interest and standing to (i) institute judicial review proceedings (and equivalent thereof in Scotland); or (ii) intervene in other legal proceedings, where it considers it appropriate to do so in order to promote the adequate and effective implementation or application of Part 2. Sub-paragraph (3) states that this will not create a new legal cause of action.

These Explanatory Notes relate to the European Union (Withdrawal Agreement) Act 2020 (c.1) which received Royal Assent on 23 January 2020

61

437 Sub-paragraph (4) defines 'application for review' in England, Wales and Northern Ireland as an application for judicial review and in Scotland as an application to the supervisory jurisdiction of the Court of Session.

Annual reports for specialised committee etc

438 Paragraph 31 places a duty on the IMA to provide annual reports on the implementation and application of Part 2 of the Withdrawal Agreement to the Specialised Committee on Citizens' Rights (which reports to the Joint Committee established to oversee the Withdrawal Agreement), and annual reports on Part 2 of the EEA EFTA Separation Agreement to the Joint Committee established by that agreement.

439 The Specialised Committee on Citizens' Rights for the Withdrawal Agreement will, under its delegated functions from the Joint Committee, be responsible for supervising the citizens' rights part of the Withdrawal Agreement. This committee will be composed of representatives from the UK and EU. It will meet at the request of either the UK or the EU and, in any event, once a year.

440 The Joint Committee for the EEA EFTA Separation Agreement will be responsible for the implementation and application of this agreement. The Joint Committee will be composed of representatives from the UK and the EEA EFTA states. It too will meet at the request of the UK or of one of the EEA states and, in any event, once a year after the end of the implementation period.

441 Sub-paragraph (3) requires the IMA's annual reports to contain information on measures taken by relevant public authorities to implement or comply with Part 2, the number and nature of complaints made, the exercise of the IMA's functions in relation to Part 2. Sub-paragraph (4) provides that the annual reports may contain any other information that the IMA considers appropriate.

442 Sub-paragraphs (5) and (6) set out the time frames the annual reports must cover. The first annual report will cover the 12-month period starting with IP completion day; subsequent reports will relate to each successive 12-month period.

443 Sub-paragraph (7) provides that the annual reports should be sent to the Specialised Committee on Citizens' Rights and the Joint Committee as soon as is reasonably practicable after the period to which they relate. At the same time, sub-paragraph (8) requires the report be sent to the Secretary of State, Scottish Ministers, Welsh Ministers and the Executive Office in Northern Ireland. This is to provide for domestic, as well as international, accountability.

444 Sub-paragraphs (9) and (10) direct the Secretary of State to lay the annual report before Parliament as soon as is practicable and to publish the report as soon as is practicable thereafter.

445 Sub-paragraph (11) directs the Scottish Ministers, Welsh Ministers and the Executive Office in Northern Ireland to lay the report before the appropriate devolved legislature as soon as is reasonably practicable after receiving it.

These Explanatory Notes relate to the European Union (Withdrawal Agreement) Act 2020 (c.1) which received Royal Assent on 23 January 2020

62

Guidance

446 Paragraph 32 requires the IMA to publish guidance on how it intends to perform its functions in relation to paragraphs 22 to 30, in particular how it will give effect to the importance of addressing general or systemic failings in the implementation and application of Part 2. In preparing the guidance, the IMA will have regard to the way the European Commission monitors and enforces citizens' rights under EU law and any guidance the Commission provides on how it exercises its functions.[9] This is in line with the requirement in Article 159 of the Withdrawal Agreement that the IMA have equivalent powers to the European Commission.

447 Sub-paragraph (4) provides that the guidance must be first published within three months of the membership of the IMA being constituted (in accordance with paragraph 2(1)).

Gibraltar

448 Paragraph 33 places a duty on the IMA to exercise any function the Gibraltar legislature confers on it, where this corresponds to a function which it has in relation to the UK. This has the effect that the IMA will only have roles and responsibilities in Gibraltar that are established through Gibraltar's legislation, as opposed to the UK legislating on Gibraltar's behalf.

Supplementary power

449 Paragraph 34 gives the IMA the power to do anything it considers necessary or expedient in relation to the exercise of its functions with the exception that the IMA will not be allowed to borrow money or accept gifts of money, land or other property.

Co-operation by relevant public authorities

450 Paragraph 35 places a duty on a relevant public authority to comply so far as is reasonably practicable with a request from the IMA to cooperate in the exercise of its functions, including any request to provide information or documents.

Part 3: Further Provisions

Disclosure of HMRC's information

451 Paragraph 36(1) permits Her Majesty's Revenue and Customs (HMRC) to disclose information for the purposes of facilitating the IMA in the exercise of its functions or facilitating the exercise by the Secretary of State or another relevant public authority of functions relating to the IMA.

452 Sub-paragraph (2) provides that where information is received by a person for the purposes set out in 36(1), they may not use the information they have received for any other purpose or disclose the information they have received except with the consent of HMRC Commissioners.

453 Sub-paragraph (3) provides that the offence of wrongful disclosure under section 19 of the Commissioners for Revenue and Customs Act 2005 will apply where a person discloses information in contravention of sub-paragraph (2) where a person's identity is specified in the disclosure or can be deduced from it. Sub-paragraph (4) clarifies that these provisions do not limit the circumstances in which information held by HMRC may be disclosed under other applicable statutes or rules of law.

---

[9] For example 'EU law: Better results through better application' https://eur-lex.europa.eu/legal-content/EN/TXT/PDF/?uri=CELEX:52017XC0119(01)&from=EN

These Explanatory Notes relate to the European Union (Withdrawal Agreement) Act 2020 (c.1) which received Royal Assent on 23 January 2020

63

Data Protection and disclosure of information

454 Paragraph 37 provides that nothing in the Schedule authorises the making of a disclosure which contravenes the Data Protection Act 2018 or the making of a disclosure which is prohibited by the Investigatory Powers Act 2016.

Prohibition on disclosure of information to IMA on national security grounds

455 Paragraph 38(1) provides a power for the Minister of the Crown to prevent a public authority from disclosing information to the IMA if the Minister of Crown determines that the disclosure would be undesirable for national security reasons. The fact as to whether or not such a determination has been made may itself be information falling within paragraph 38(1).

456 Sub-paragraph (2) states that the power under sub-paragraph (1) conferred on a Minister of the Crown is exercisable only by a Minister who is a member of the Cabinet, or the Attorney General or the Advocate General for Scotland.

Transfer of IMA's functions and abolition

457 Paragraph 39(1) provides a power for the Secretary of State to make regulations to transfer the functions of the IMA to another public authority, and make modifications to that authority that the Secretary of State considers appropriate to ensure they possess appropriate functions, funding and constitutional arrangements. 'Constitutional arrangements' has the same meaning as that in section 3(2) of the Public Bodies Act 2011. This will allow the Secretary of State to ensure that the transferee possesses the functions required by Article 159 of the Withdrawal Agreement, as well as having the resources and constitutional design necessary to fulfil this role.

458 Sub-paragraph (2) ensures that the Secretary of State can only use the power under sub-paragraph (1) if they are satisfied that the transfer of the IMA's functions to another public authority would improve the exercise of those functions, having regard to efficiency, effectiveness and economy.

459 Sub-paragraph (3) requires the Secretary of State to have regard to the need to ensure that any public authority to which the IMA's functions are transferred under sub-paragraph (1) has operational independence and the ability to make impartial assessments when exercising the transferred functions, as well as appropriate funding to do so

460 Sub-paragraph (4) prevents the power under sub-paragraph (1) from being used to transfer the IMA's functions in respect of Gibraltar under paragraph 33. Consequently, the Gibraltar legislature will need to confer the IMA's functions on the public authority to which they have been transferred under sub-paragraph (1), if these functions are to continue to have effect in Gibraltar.

461 Sub-paragraph (5)(a) provides for the Secretary of State to transfer the IMA's property, rights and liabilities, including those in respect of contracts of employment, under sub-paragraph (1). sub-paragraph (5)(b) provides for the Secretary of State to abolish the IMA under sub-paragraph (1), once this power has been exercised and the IMA's functions have been transferred to a different public authority.

462 Sub-paragraph (6) places a duty on the Secretary of State to consult the Scottish Minister, the Welsh Ministers, the Executive Office in Northern Ireland, and the Gibraltar Ministers if the IMA has functions in relation to Gibraltar by virtue of paragraph 33.

463 Sub-paragraph (7) enables regulations made under sub-paragraph (1) to modify any provision made by or under an enactment, including this Act.

These Explanatory Notes relate to the European Union (Withdrawal Agreement) Act 2020 (c.1) which received Royal Assent on 23 January 2020

64

464 Sub-paragraph (8) states that 'constitutional arrangements' as used in sub-paragraph (1) has the same meaning as that in section 3(2) of the Public Bodies Act 2011.

465 Paragraph 40(1) provides a power for the Secretary of State to make regulations to either modify the functions of the IMA, or abolish the IMA, if it appears, or having regard to the Withdrawal Agreement and the EEA EFTA Separation Agreement and the relevant provisions of such agreements that concern the ending of the IMA's functions, that it is no longer necessary for the IMA to exercise functions in relation to Part 2 of the Withdrawal Agreement. This is to reflect the respective Joint Committees' power under the agreements to decide that the IMA's functions are no longer required.

466 The Secretary of State may also make regulations for the IMA to cease to exist where, having regard to the Withdrawal Agreement and EEA EFTA Separation Agreement, it is no longer needed. As set out in Article 159 of the Withdrawal Agreement and Article 64 of the EEA EFTA Separation Agreement, the joint committees may decide to bring the IMA to an end from eight years after the end of the implementation period.

467 Sub-paragraph (2) enables regulations made under sub-paragraph (1) to modify any provision made by or under an enactment, including this Act.

Interpretation

468 Paragraph 41 defines 'civil servant' as a person employed in the civil service of the state, and sets out the definition for 'domestic law'. The term 'devolved legislature' is defined as the Scottish Parliament, the National Assembly of Wales or the Northern Ireland Assembly. The terms 'Part 2' and 'relevant public authority' are defined under sub-paragraph 22(3).

469 A 'relevant right' means a right created or arising under Part 2 of the Withdrawal Agreement or Part 2 of the EEA EFTA Separation Agreement (for example the right to apply for permanent residency if the criteria set out in Part 2 are met). It includes any right arising under Part 2, regardless of the legal means through which that right is given effect - it covers both rights that exist in Part 2 and are made directly effectively through this Act (by virtue of sections 5 and 6) and rights that result from the obligations on the UK created by Part 2, but which are given further effect by domestic law (for example, the settled status scheme created under the Immigration Rules). It also includes rights which 'correspond' to rights created or arising under Part 2 (but which are not in fact conferred by Part 2) and which are established in domestic legislation which has effect in connection with Part 2. For example, where the settled status scheme is extended to EU or EEA nationals not strictly in the scope of the relevant agreements and those people are accordingly given associated rights such as non-discrimination rights corresponding to those conferred on people directly covered by Part 2, those corresponding rights fall within the definition of 'relevant right'.

470 Sub-paragraph (2) sets out that any references referring to relevant public authorities acting include references to the relevant public authority failing to act.

Schedule 3: Protection for certain rights, safeguards etc in Belfast Agreement

471 The purpose of Schedule 3 is to make provision for the 'no diminution' commitment and the arrangements necessary for the 'dedicated mechanisms' required under Article 2(1) of the Protocol on Ireland/Northern Ireland. That Article states that there is to be no diminution of rights, safeguards and equality of opportunity as set out in the 'Rights, Safeguards and Equality of Opportunity' chapter of the Belfast (Good Friday) Agreement 1998 in Northern Ireland resulting from the UK's withdrawal from the EU, including in the area of protection against discrimination enshrined in the provisions of EU law listed in Annex 1 to the Protocol. This is to be implemented by way of 'dedicated mechanisms'.

These Explanatory Notes relate to the European Union (Withdrawal Agreement) Act 2020 (c.1) which received Royal Assent on 23 January 2020

65

472 Paragraph 1 highlights that the subsequent sections make amendments to the Northern Ireland Act 1998.

473 Paragraphs 2 and 3 of Schedule 3 contain the following amendments to the Northern Ireland Act 1998:

    a.   paragraph 2 inserts a fetter into section 6(2) of the Northern Ireland Act 1998, which prevents the Northern Ireland Assembly from legislating incompatibly with Article 2(1) of the Protocol;

    b.   paragraph 3 inserts a fetter into section 24(1) of the Northern Ireland Act 1998 which prevents Northern Ireland Ministers and departments from acting in a way which is incompatible with Article 2(1) of the Protocol.

474 Paragraphs 4 and 6 insert new subsections into section 69 and 74 of the Northern Ireland Act 1998 respectively, signposting to the new sections of that Act which set out the new functions and powers of the Northern Ireland Human Rights Commission (NIHRC) and the Equality Commission for Northern Ireland (ECNI) as part of the 'dedicated mechanisms', as required under Article 2(1) of the Protocol.

475 Paragraph 5 amends section 71 of the Northern Ireland Act 1998 to clarify the NIHRC's 'own motion' standing powers to challenge the compatibility of legislation with the European Convention on Human Rights, via the Human Rights Act 1998. The combined effect of these amendments is that the criteria and restrictions set out in section 71(2B)(a)-(d) do not apply where the NIHRC brings these proceedings under section 69(5)(b) (proceedings involving law or practice relating to the protection of human rights) and the NIHRC will be able to bring these proceedings without being required to show that there would be an actual or potential victim.

476 Paragraph 7 inserts new sections 78A to 78E into the Northern Ireland Act 1998 which set out the functions the NIHRC and ECNI will have as part of the dedicated mechanism.

Section 78A - NIHRC functions in relation to EU withdrawal agreement

477 New section 78A of the Northern Ireland Act 1998 sets out the functions of the NIHRC as part of the dedicated mechanism.

478 The NIHRC will be required to monitor the implementation of Article 2(1) of the Protocol (78A(1)). It will also be required to report to the Secretary of State and the Executive Office in Northern Ireland on the implementation of Article 2(1) of the Protocol (78A(2)) and may require them to reply to such a report and explain what steps they have taken, or are planning to take, in response to any recommendation/s contained in the report (78A(3)). Where the NIHRC makes such a report under subsection (3), the Secretary of State must lay a copy of that report before Parliament and the Executive Office must lay a copy of it before the Assembly (78A(4)).

479 This section also includes a duty to advise the Secretary of State and the Executive Committee of the Assembly of legislative and other measures that ought to be taken to implement the commitment in Article 2(1) (78A(5)). The NIHRC is also required to advise the Assembly on the compatibility of proposed Assembly legislation with Article 2(1) of the Protocol (78A(6)) and to promote understanding and awareness of the importance of Article 2(1) through research and educational activities (78A(7)). This section also allows the NIHRC to publish its advice and the outcome of its research (78A(8)) and to bring any appropriate matters to the attention of the Specialised Committee referred to in Article 14(c) of the Protocol (78A(9)).

These Explanatory Notes relate to the European Union (Withdrawal Agreement) Act 2020 (c.1) which received Royal Assent on 23 January 2020

66

Section 78B - ECNI functions in relation to EU withdrawal agreement

480 New section 78B of the Northern Ireland Act 1998 sets out the functions of the ECNI as part of the dedicated mechanism, which are the same as the functions of the NIHRC in relation to Article 2(1) of the Protocol.

481 The ECNI will be required to monitor the implementation of Article 2(1) of the Protocol (78B(1)). It will also be required to report to the Secretary of State and the Executive Office in Northern Ireland on the implementation of Article 2(1) of the Protocol (78B(2)); and may require them to reply to such a report and explain what steps they have taken, or are planning to take, in response to any recommendation/s contained in the report (78B(3)). Where the ECNI makes such a report under subsection (3), the Secretary of State must lay a copy of it before Parliament and the Executive Office must lay a copy of it before the Assembly (78B(4)).

482 This section also includes a duty to advise the Secretary of State and the Executive Committee of the Assembly of legislative and other measures which ought to be taken to implement the commitment in Article 2(1) (78B(5)). The ECNI is also required to advise the Assembly on the compatibility of proposed Assembly legislation with Article 2(1) of the Protocol (78B(6)) and to promote understanding and awareness of the importance of Article 2(1) through research and educational activities (78B(7)). This section also allows the ECNI to publish its advice and the outcome of its research (78B(8)) and to bring any appropriate matters to the attention of the Specialised Committee referred to in Article 14(c) of the Protocol (78B(9)).

Section 78C - Power of Commissions to bring, or intervene in, legal proceedings

483 This section provides that both the NIHRC and the ECNI can bring judicial proceedings, in respect of an alleged breach (or potential future breach) of Article 2(1) of the Protocol. The NIHRC and ECNI can also intervene in legal proceedings in so far as they relate to an alleged breach (or potential future breach) of Article 2(1) of the Protocol. Subsection (2) clarifies that this does not create a new cause of action.

Section 78D - Power of Commissions to assist persons in legal proceedings

484 This section enables the NIHRC and ECNI to assist a person in proceedings, or proposed proceedings, in so far they relate to an alleged breach (or potential future breach) of Article 2(1) of the Protocol.

485 Subsection (2) lays out the situations in which the NIHRC and ECNI can grant an application for assistance, namely where the proceedings in question raise a question of principle, where it would be unreasonable to expect a person to pursue the proceedings without assistance due to their complexity, because of the person's position in relation to another person involved or for some other reason, or where there are other special circumstances which make it appropriate for the NIHRC or ECNI to provide assistance.

486 Subsection (3) states that where the NIHRC or ECNI grants an application for assistance, it can provide or arrange for the provision of legal advice; arrange for the provision of legal representation; and provide any other assistance which it thinks is appropriate.

487 Subsection (4) provides that arrangements made for the provision of assistance may include provision to recover expenses from the person in certain circumstances.

Section 78E - Collaborative working

488 This section states that the NIHRC and ECNI can arrange for any of their functions under the above sections to be carried out either by acting jointly or by one of them acting on behalf of the other.

These Explanatory Notes relate to the European Union (Withdrawal Agreement) Act 2020 (c.1) which received Royal Assent on 23 January 2020

67

489 Paragraph 8 of Schedule 3 of this Act adds the new sections 78A to 78E to the list of reserved matters contained in paragraph 42 of Schedule 3 of the Northern Ireland Act 1998, meaning that the Northern Ireland Assembly would only be able to legislate for the matters to which those sections relate with the consent of the Secretary of State.

Schedule 4: Regulations under this Act

Part 1: Procedure

490 Part 1 of this Schedule sets out the parliamentary procedures attaching to the regulations laid under the various powers in the Act.

491 Sub-paragraphs 1(1) and (2) set out the procedures for regulations under section 7 (rights related to residence: deadline for applications and temporary protection); section 8 (frontier workers); and section 9 (restrictions of rights of entry and residence). Sub-paragraph 1(1) provides that the first regulations under section 7(1)(b) to (g), 8(1), or 9, and regulations under section 7, 8 or 9 which amend repeal or revoke primary legislation or retained direct principal EU legislation are subject to the draft affirmative procedure. Sub-paragraph (2) provides that any other regulations made under section 7, 8 or 9 shall be subject to the negative resolution procedure.

492 Sub-paragraph 2(1) sets out the procedure that will apply to the first regulations made under section 11 (appeals against citizens' rights immigration decisions). The procedure that shall apply to the first set of regulations made under section 11 is the made affirmative procedure. Sub-paragraph (2) provides that subsequent regulations made under section 11 that amend repeal or revoke primary legislation or retained direct principal EU legislation are subject to the draft affirmative procedure. Sub-paragraph (3) provides that any other regulation made under section 11 is subject to the negative resolution procedure. Sub-paragraphs (4) and (5) set out in further detail the operation of the made affirmative procedure.

493 Sub-paragraphs 3(1) and (2) set out the procedures that apply to regulations made by a Minister of the Crown acting alone under section 12 (recognition of professional qualifications); section 13 (co-ordination of social security systems); and section 14 (non-discrimination, equal treatment and rights of workers etc). Sub-paragraph (1) provides that regulations made by a Minister of the Crown acting alone under sections 12, 13, or 14 that amend, repeal or revoke primary legislation or retained direct principal EU legislation are subject to the draft affirmative procedure. Sub-paragraph (2) provides that any other regulations made by a Minister of the Crown acting alone under sections 12, 13, or 14 are subject to the negative resolution procedure.

494 Sub-paragraphs (3) and (4) set out the procedures that apply to regulations made by a Scottish Minister acting alone under section 12 (recognition of professional qualifications); section 13 (co-ordination of social security systems); and section 14 (non-discrimination, equal treatment and rights of workers etc). Sub-paragraph (3) provides that regulations made by a Scottish Minister acting alone under section 12, 13, or 14 that amend, repeal, or revoke primary legislation or retained direct principal EU legislation are subject to the draft affirmative procedure. Sub-paragraph (4) provides that other regulations made by a Scottish Minister acting alone under section 12, 13, or 14 are subject to the negative resolution procedure.

These Explanatory Notes relate to the European Union (Withdrawal Agreement) Act 2020 (c.1) which received Royal Assent on 23 January 2020

68

495 Sub-paragraphs (5) and (6) set out the procedures that apply to regulations made by a Welsh Minister acting alone under section 12 (recognition of professional qualifications); section 13 (co-ordination of social security systems); and section 14 (non-discrimination, equal treatment and rights of workers etc). Sub-paragraph (5) provides that regulations made by a Welsh Minister acting alone under section 12, 13, or 14 that amend, repeal, or revoke primary legislation or retained direct principal EU legislation are subject to the draft affirmative procedure. Sub-paragraph (6) provides that other regulations made by a Welsh Minister acting alone under section 12, 13, or 14 are subject to the negative resolution procedure.

496 Sub-paragraphs (7) and (8) set out the procedures that apply to regulations made by a Northern Ireland department acting alone under section 12 (recognition of professional qualifications); section 13 (co-ordination of social security systems); and section 14 (non-discrimination, equal treatment and rights of workers etc). Sub-paragraph (7) provides that regulations made by a Northern Ireland department acting alone under section 12, 13, or 14 that amend, repeal, or revoke primary legislation or retained direct principal EU legislation are subject to the draft affirmative procedure. Sub-paragraph (8) provides that other regulations made by a Northern Ireland department acting alone under section 12, 13, or 14 are subject to the negative resolution procedure.

497 Paragraph 4 sets out the procedures that apply to regulations made under section 12 (recognition of professional qualifications); section 13 (co-ordination of social security systems); and section 14 (non-discrimination, equal treatment and rights of workers etc) by a Minister of the Crown acting jointly with a devolved authority. In addition to the other application procedures provided for under paragraph 4 regulations made by a Minister of the Crown acting jointly with a devolved authority that amend, repeal, or revoke primary legislation or retained direct principal EU legislation are subject to the draft affirmative procedure by resolution of each House of Parliament. Any other regulations made jointly are subject to the negative procedure by resolution of either House of Parliament.

498 Paragraph 5 sets out the procedure that applies to regulations made under section 39(4) to amend the definition of 'IP completion day' to take account of changes to EU summertime. Any such regulations will be subject to the negative resolution procedure.

499 Paragraph 6 establishes that regulations made under section 41(1) to make consequential provision are to be made under the negative procedure.

500 Paragraph 7 sets out the procedure that applies to regulations made under paragraph 39 or 40 of Schedule 2 (transfer and abolition of IMA's functions), which is the draft affirmative procedure.

501 Paragraph 8 applies to the power in paragraph 1(3) of Schedule 5 of the Act which allows a Minister of the Crown or devolved authority acting alone to make exceptions from the mass deferral. Where a Minister of the Crown, the Scottish Ministers, Welsh Ministers or a Northern Ireland department are exercising these powers before exit day, the regulations will be subject to no procedure. Where the powers are being exercised on or after exit day, the regulations will be subject to the negative procedure.

502 Paragraph 9 applies to the power in paragraph 1(3) of Schedule 5 of the Act where it is being exercised jointly by a Minister of the Crown and a devolved authority. Where the powers are exercised jointly before exit day, the regulations will be subject to no procedure. Where the powers are being exercised jointly on or after exit day, the regulations will be subject to the negative procedure. A statutory instrument containing regulations is subject to the negative procedure by resolution of either House of Parliament as well as any other applicable procedure under paragraph 9.

These Explanatory Notes relate to the European Union (Withdrawal Agreement) Act 2020 (c.1) which received Royal Assent on 23 January 2020

69

503 Paragraph 10 sets out that regulations made on or after exit day by Scottish Ministers, Welsh Ministers or Northern Ireland departments under paragraph 3(2) of Schedule 5 are subject to the negative procedure in the respective legislatures.

Part 2: General provision about powers under Act

504 Part 2 of Schedule 4 makes general provision in respect of the scope and nature of the powers contained in the Act.

505 Paragraph 11 provides that powers to make regulations in the Act are exercisable by statutory instrument (where exercised by a Minister of the Crown alone, by a Minister of the Crown acting jointly with a devolved authority, or by a Welsh minister acting alone or jointly with a Minister of the Crown) and by statutory rule (where the powers are exercised by a Northern Ireland department alone). Regulations made by Scottish ministers acting alone will be made by Scottish statutory instrument, as provided for by section 27 of the Interpretation and Legislative Reform (Scotland) Act 2010.

506 Paragraph 12 clarifies the scope of the powers in the Act by providing that all the powers in the Act can be used to make different provision for different cases or descriptions of case, in different circumstances, areas or for different purposes and include the power to make supplementary etc provision.

507 Paragraph 13 provides that powers in the Act may overlap without that overlap impacting on the scope of each of the powers.

508 Paragraph 14 clarifies that powers in the Act relating to the Agreements can be exercised before the Agreements are ratified so that the regulations can come into force on or after the day the Agreements are ratified. This also includes any modifications of those agreements that require ratification.

509 Paragraph 15 clarifies that the power for Ministers to commence certain parts of the Act, as provided for by section 42(7), includes the power to specify the time of day these parts of the Act come into force.

510 Paragraph 16 sets out that regulations brought forward under the powers in this Act are never to be treated as hybrid instruments. Some statutory instruments which need to be approved by both Houses (affirmative instruments) are ruled to be hybrid instruments because they affect some members of a group (be it individuals or bodies) in a manner different from others in the same group.

511 Paragraph 17 makes provision for the applicable procedure when instruments containing regulations made under this Act are combined.

Schedule 5: Consequential, transitional and saving provision

Part 1: General consequential provision

512 As set out in the Withdrawal Agreement, the UK will stay closely aligned with the EU for the duration of the implementation period, from exit day until IP completion day. The Act therefore makes provision for subordinate legislation which deals with the UK's withdrawal from the EU (sometimes known as 'EU exit SIs'), to come into force by reference to IP completion day, so that domestic law does not diverge from EU law during the implementation period.

These Explanatory Notes relate to the European Union (Withdrawal Agreement) Act 2020 (c.1) which received Royal Assent on 23 January 2020

70

513 Paragraph 1(1) of this Schedule contains a general rule that 'glosses' (i.e. non-textually amends) the commencement dates in subordinate legislation made before exit day. The gloss will apply to subordinate legislation made under the EU (Withdrawal) Act 2018 or any other enactment, including where made under a sub-delegated power. The gloss will apply to subordinate legislation, which is due to come into force on, immediately before or after exit day (such as 'three months after exit day'). This subordinate legislation will instead come into force at the end of the implementation period, either immediately before, on, or after IP completion day (such as 'three months after IP completion day').

514 The general rule will apply where the commencement date relates to all or part of that subordinate legislation or any other subordinate legislation which it provides for. It will therefore apply to either:

   a. all of that subordinate legislation if the commencement date for all of that subordinate legislation is exit day (or immediately before or at any time after exit day, where it is by reference to exit day);

   b. particular provisions of that subordinate legislation if there are different commencement dates for different provisions, with some entering into force on exit day (or immediately before or at any time after exit day, where it is by reference to exit day), and others entering into force on a different date; or

   c. none of that subordinate legislation if none of the provisions of come into force on exit day (or immediately before or at any time after exit day, where it is by reference to exit day).

515 As such, the general rule will not affect provisions in subordinate legislation that do not come into force on exit day (or immediately before or at any time after exit day, where it is by reference to exit day). Further, whilst the general rule will bite on references to exit day 'however expressed', it will not bite on provisions which happen to commence on that day and/or time.

516 Paragraph 1(2) allows subordinate legislation to expressly disapply this gloss where required. This means regulations requiring exception that are laid alongside the Act, or between the Act passing and exit day, may be able to specifically provide for this.

517 Paragraph 1(3) contains a power for an appropriate authority (as defined in paragraph 1(6)) to make exceptions to the mass deferral, by disapplying or making different provision from the mass deferral in particular cases. For example, a Minister of the Crown, devolved authority or Minister of the Crown acting jointly with a devolved authority could exempt regulations fixing a deficiency under section 8(1) of the EU (Withdrawal) Act 2018 from the mass deferral, to provide that they will still come into force on exit day, where this is deemed appropriate.

518 Paragraph 1(4) refers the user to paragraph 2 of this Schedule for further provision about the power of devolved authorities to make regulations under paragraph 1(3).

519 Paragraph 1(5) sunsets the use of the power in paragraph 1(3) at one year after IP completion day, defined as 31 December 2020 at 11.00 p.m. in section 39.

520 Paragraph 1(6) defines 'appropriate authority' as a Minister of the Crown, a devolved authority or a Minister of the Crown acting jointly with a devolved authority.

These Explanatory Notes relate to the European Union (Withdrawal Agreement) Act 2020 (c.1) which received Royal Assent on 23 January 2020

71

521 Paragraph 2 provides that a devolved authority acting alone under the power in paragraph 1(3) may make regulations that make different provisions for particular cases from the mass deferral or provide for the mass deferral to not apply where the devolved authority made the provision commencing the subordinate legislation to be excepted and, if so, would otherwise have the power to provide for the same effect as the exception (or they did so in the original instrument which is to be subject to the exception); or, if not, in cases where the devolved authority would have the power acting alone to make the commencement provision and the substantive subordinate legislation to be subject to the exception. Paragraph 2 also provides that a devolved authority may not make provision under paragraph 1(3) relating to the coming into force of regulations under section 23(1) or (6) of, or paragraph 1(2)(b) of Schedule 1 to the EU (Withdrawal) Act 2018. In certain cases where the devolved authority would otherwise have required the consent of a Minister of the Crown to make the provision under paragraph 1(3), such consent is also required for the devolved authority to exercise the power under paragraph 1(3). In all other cases, a devolved authority may not make provision under paragraph 1(3) unless they have consulted a Minister of the Crown.

522 Paragraph 3 makes the same provision as paragraph 1 but for primary legislation made by devolved authorities in preparation for exit day under the provisions in paragraph 41(3) to (5) of Schedule 8 to the EU (Withdrawal) Act 2018. Those provisions were commenced after the Supreme Court judgment in 'The UK Withdrawal from the European Union (Legal Continuity) (Scotland) Act' reference, which decided that the Scottish Parliament had competence to legislate in preparation for EU exit because the requirement to legislate compatibly with EU law would cease on a specific date. The provisions in this Act include the gloss of 'exit day' to 'IP completion day'; the power to disapply or make different provision to the deferral; as well as the power to make appropriate provision, including re-stating the commencement date of such an enactment. sub-paragraphs (3) to (6) clarify that these powers can modify provisions in primary legislation as well as secondary legislation and that devolved authorities cannot use it outside of legislative competence.

523 Paragraph 4(1) clarifies that the consequential power in section 23(1) of the EU (Withdrawal) Act 2018 is capable of making consequential provision on the Act as amended (or to be amended) by or under the Act. Further, it clarifies that references in the EU (Withdrawal) Act 2018 to the consequential power are read accordingly. Sub-paragraph (2) clarifies that sub-paragraph (1) does not limit the scope of the consequential power in section 41(1) of this Act. Sub-paragraph (3) clarifies that this includes amendments to provisions of the EU (Withdrawal) Act 2018 which make amendments to other legislation.

Part 2: Specific Consequential Provision

Interpretation Act (Northern Ireland) 1954 (c.33 (NI))

524 Paragraphs 5 to 7 amend the Interpretation Act (Northern Ireland) 1954 to reflect that the UK will enter an implementation period after exit day.

525 Paragraph 5 introduces the amendments to the Interpretation Act (Northern Ireland) 1954.

526 Paragraph 6 amends section 11 of that Act to substitute all references to 'exit day' in subsections (1C), (1D) and (1E) to read instead 'IP completion day'.

527 Paragraph 7 amends section 44A of that Act, concerning definitions relating to the UK's withdrawal from the EU, to insert definitions for 'EU withdrawal agreement' and 'IP completion day'. It also substitutes the reference to 'exit day' in the definition of 'retained EU obligation' to read instead 'IP completion day'.

These Explanatory Notes relate to the European Union (Withdrawal Agreement) Act 2020 (c.1) which received Royal Assent on 23 January 2020

72

Interpretation Act 1978

528 Paragraphs 8 to 12 amend the Interpretation Act 1978 to reflect that the UK will enter an implementation period after exit day.

529 Paragraph 8 introduces the amendments to the Interpretation Act.

530 Paragraph 9 amends section 20(3) (references to other enactments) of the Interpretation Act which will be inserted by the European Union (Withdrawal) Act 2018 (Consequential Modifications and Repeals and Revocations) (EU Exit) Regulations 2018. Section 20(3) of the Interpretation Act will make interpretative provision for references on or after exit day to EU instruments which form part of domestic law by virtue of section 3 of the EU (Withdrawal) Act 2018. This will be amended to instead provide for references on or after IP completion day.

531 Paragraph 10 amends the definition of subordinate legislation in section 21(1) of the Interpretation Act to include instruments of the same nature made on or after IP completion day under any retained direct EU legislation. Paragraph 19 of Schedule 8 to the EU (Withdrawal) Act 2018 amended the definition to include such instruments made on or after exit day. In light of direct EU legislation being retained on IP completion day, paragraph 7 of this Schedule amends this definition so it refers to IP completion day instead.

532 Paragraph 11 amends section 23ZA(4)(a)(ii) of the Interpretation Act, which is inserted into the Act by paragraph 20 of Schedule 8 of the EU (Withdrawal) Act 2018. This means the definition of 'commencement' in Schedule 1 of the Interpretation Act will apply to instruments made under any retained direct EU legislation on or after IP completion day rather than exit day. As such, where legislation refers to the commencement of these instruments (and the Interpretation Act definition applies) it means the time when the instrument comes into force.

533 Paragraph 12 adds a number of definitions to Schedule 1 to the Interpretation Act. It adds definitions for the 'EU withdrawal agreement' and 'IP completion day' (which have the same meaning as provided for in the Act). Further, it amends the definition of 'retained EU obligation' so that it refers to IP completion day rather than exit day, to reflect that retained EU law will not be preserved until IP completion day. It also amends the definition of 'EU Treaties' or 'the EU Treaties' so that it refers to the treaties that apply under the saved ECA immediately before IP completion day.

European Economic Area Act 1993

534 Paragraphs 13 to 16 make technical amendments to changes to the European Economic Area Act 1993 made by the EU (Withdrawal) Act 2018. These amendments are necessary as the existing international agreements between the UK and the EEA EFTA states will be preserved for the duration of the implementation period.

535 Paragraphs 14 and 15 amend section 2 and 3 of the European Economic Area Act. These sections ensure that domestic legislation that was in force prior to the entry into force of the EEA Agreement in 1993 is read consistently with the provisions of that Agreement. Paragraphs 14 and 15 ensure that the modifications made to sections 2 and 3 will continue to operate appropriately in light of the implementation period.

536 Paragraph 16 makes a consequential amendment to section 6 of the European Economic Area Act in light of the temporary saving of the ECA.

These Explanatory Notes relate to the European Union (Withdrawal Agreement) Act 2020 (c.1) which received Royal Assent on 23 January 2020

73

Scotland Act 1998

537 Paragraphs 17 to 21 make technical amendments to changes to the Scotland Act 1998 made by the EU (Withdrawal) Act 2018 to reflect that the UK will remain aligned with EU law for the duration of the implementation period. Paragraph 20 sets out the amendments made by this Act to the EU (Withdrawal) Act 2018 that are not protected from modification.

Northern Ireland Act 1998

538 Paragraphs 22, 23, 25 and 26 make technical amendments to changes to the Northern Ireland Act 1998 made by the EU (Withdrawal) Act 2018 to reflect that the UK will remain aligned with EU law for the duration of the implementation period.

539 Paragraph 24 sets out the amendments made by this Act to the EU (Withdrawal) Act 2018 that are excluded from entrenchment.

Government of Wales Act 2006

540 Paragraphs 27 to 30 make technical amendments to changes to the Government of Wales Act 2006 made by the EU (Withdrawal) Act 2018 to reflect that the UK will remain aligned with EU law for the duration of the implementation period. Paragraph 31 sets out the amendments made by this Act to the EU (Withdrawal) Act 2018 that are not protected from modification.

Interpretation and Legislative Reform (Scotland) Act 2010 (asp 10)

541 Paragraphs 32 to 37 amend the Interpretation and Legislative Reform (Scotland) Act 2010 ('ILRA').

542 Paragraph 32 introduces amendments to the ILRA.

543 Paragraph 33 amends the changes made by the EU (Withdrawal) Act 2018 to the definition of 'Scottish instruments' in Part 1 of the ILRA. This ensures that the various rules of interpretation in Part 1 of the ILRA will apply to instruments made after IP completion day, rather than exit day, under a combination of powers in an Act of the Scottish Parliament and in retained direct EU legislation.

544 Paragraph 34 amends changes made by the European Union (Withdrawal) Act 2018 (Consequential Modifications and Repeals and Revocations) (EU Exit) Regulations 2018 to section 14 ILRA. This ensures that there is interpretative provision for references on or after IP completion day to EU instruments which form part of domestic law by virtue of section 3 of the EU (Withdrawal) Act 2018.

545 Paragraph 35 amends changes made by paragraph 33 of Schedule 8 to the EU Withdrawal Act 2018. It omits an obsolete reference to Regulations made under Part 2 of Schedule 2 of the EU Withdrawal Act 2018. Part 2 of Schedule 2 (implementing the withdrawal agreement) of EUWA is repealed by section 36 (repeal of unnecessary or spent enactments) of the EU (Withdrawal Agreement) Act 2020.

546 Paragraph 36 amends changes made by the European Union (Withdrawal) Act 2018 (Consequential Modifications and Repeals and Revocations) (EU Exit) Regulations 2018 to section 55 ILRA. This ensures that definitions within the Scotland Act 1998 (Transitory and Transitional Provisions) (Publication and Interpretation etc of Acts of the Scottish Parliament) Order 1999 (S.I. 1999/1379) reflect the Withdrawal Agreement and Act.

547 Paragraph 37 amends changes made to the definitions in Schedule 1 of the ILRA by the EU (Withdrawal) Act 2018 and the European Union (Withdrawal) Act 2018 (Consequential Modifications and Repeals and Revocations) (EU Exit) Regulations 2018. This ensures that the definitions reflect the Withdrawal Agreement and Act.

These Explanatory Notes relate to the European Union (Withdrawal Agreement) Act 2020 (c.1) which received Royal Assent on 23 January 2020

74

548 Paragraph 38 introduces a further set of amendments to the EU (Withdrawal) Act 2018.

549 Paragraph 39 amends the heading above section 2 of that Act from 'existing EU law' to 'saved EU law at the end of implementation period'.

550 Paragraph 40 amends section 7 of that Act, on the status of retained EU law, as follows:

    a.   sub-paragraph (1) introduces the amendments to come;

    b.   sub-paragraph (2) amends section 7(1) of that Act so that it refers instead to the savings made on exit day by sections 1A(2) and 1B(2) of the revised Act. The amended section 7(1) then clarifies that the ECA and EU-derived legislation will continue as legislation of the same type as they were before exit day;

    c.   sub-paragraph (3) inserts new subsection (1A), which clarifies that any EU-derived domestic legislation that is saved by section 2 of the Act will continue as legislation of the same type as it was before IP completion day;

    d.   sub-paragraph (4) amends section 7(5) of that Act, which signposts provisions about the status of retained EU law in other provisions of the Act, to reflect other amendments to the Act; and

    e.   sub-paragraph (5) amends references to 'exit day' to 'IP completion day' to reflect that retained direct EU legislation will be retained on IP completion day instead of exit day.

551 Sub-paragraphs 41(1) and 41(2) amends the heading before section 10 of the EU (Withdrawal) Act 2018, whilst sub-paragraph 41(3) amends section 10 to protect the Belfast (Good Friday) Agreement 1998 without reference to its definition in section 98 of the Northern Ireland Act 1998.

552 Paragraph 42 amends the heading and text for section 11 of the EU (Withdrawal) Act 2018, in consequence of the devolved authorities being granted corresponding powers to sections 8B, and 8C and the repeal of section 9.

553 Paragraph 43 changes the heading in section 13 to reflect the insertion of new section 13A. Paragraph 43 changes the heading at section 13 from 'approval of outcome of EU negotiations' to 'oversight of withdrawal'.

554 Paragraph 44 amends section 20 of the EU (Withdrawal) Act 2018:

    a.   paragraph 44(1) introduces the amendments to that section;

    b.   paragraph 44(2) amends section (20)(1):

        i.   paragraph 44(2)(a) inserts a definition of 'Commons sitting day';

        ii.   paragraph 44(2)(b) amends the definition of 'domestic law', so that the references in new section 7A and 7B refer to the law of England and Wales, Scotland and Northern Ireland;

        iii.   paragraph 44(2)(c) amends the definition of 'enactment' so that references to this in new section 1B of the EU (Withdrawal) Act 2018 will not include retained direct EU legislation;

        iv.   paragraph 44(2)(d) inserts a definition of 'Joint Committee' and 'Lords sitting day';

These Explanatory Notes relate to the European Union (Withdrawal Agreement) Act 2020 (c.1) which received Royal Assent on 23 January 2020

75

v.   paragraph 44(2)(e) inserts a definition of 'ratify';

vi.   paragraph 44(2)(f) amends the definition of 'retained direct EU legislation' so that it refers to IP completion day rather than exit day;

vii.   paragraph 44(2)(g) amends the definition of 'subordinate legislation', so that it refers to IP completion day rather than exit day; and

viii.   paragraph 44(2)(h) removes the definition of the Withdrawal Agreement currently in that section of the EU (Withdrawal) Act 2018.

c.   Paragraph 44(3) inserts a new subsection 5A into section 20 of that Act. New subsection 5A(a) makes clear that any references to anything that continues to be law by virtue of section 1B(2) (the saving of EU-derived domestic legislation for the implementation period) includes modifications to that legislation from time to time. Subsection 5A also acknowledges that some of the legislation 'saved' by new section 1B would survive repeal of the ECA and withdrawal from the EU in any event. Subsection 5A(b) provides that references in the Act to things which continue to be domestic law, includes things which would have continued to exist regardless of the saving in new section 1B(2). This makes clear that it is not necessary to consider whether an enactment might have been subject to implied repeal or revocation on exit day, in order to bring it within the ambit of new section 1B(2).

d.   Paragraph 44(4) amends section 20(6) of the EU (Withdrawal) Act 2018 so as to amend the reference to 'exit day' in that section to read 'IP completion day'. This makes clear that it is not necessary to consider whether an enactment might have been subject to implied repeal or revocation on IP completion day, to bring it within the ambit of section 2 of the Act and the definition of 'retained EU law'.

555 Paragraph 45 amends section 21(1) (index of defined expressions) of the EU (Withdrawal) Act 2018. Section 21 lists various expressions used throughout the Act and the corresponding provision at which their meaning is located. For ease of reference, the index also includes pointers to certain provisions in the Interpretation Act 1978 (i.e. those which are restated by the Act). The Interpretation Act 1978 contains other definitions which are also relevant to the Act. Paragraph 45 amends the index at section 21 to include the new definitions in the amended Act and the corresponding provision at which their meaning is located.

556 Paragraph 46 amends section 23 of the EU (Withdrawal) Act 2018 on consequential and transitional provisions:

a.   paragraph 46(1) introduces the amendments;

b.   paragraph 46(2) amends section 23(3) so to provide that Ministers cannot make consequential provision which amends primary legislation (or secondary legislation made under that primary legislation) passed after IP completion day;

c.   paragraph 46(3) amends section 23(4) to make clear that the temporary power in subsection (1) can only be used for up to ten years after IP completion day as it expires at that point;

d.   paragraph 46(4) amends section 23(6) so that the transitional, transitory and savings power can make provision in connection with the coming into force date of any provision of the Act including its operation in connection with IP completion day.

These Explanatory Notes relate to the European Union (Withdrawal Agreement) Act 2020 (c.1) which received Royal Assent on 23 January 2020

76

557 Paragraph 47 amends Schedule 4 (powers in connection with fees and charges):

a. paragraph 47(1) introduces the amendments to Schedule 4;

b. paragraph 47(2) amends paragraph 1(1) of Schedule 4 to remove the power to provide for fees and charges in relation to section 9 and Part 2 of Schedule 2 to the EU (Withdrawal) Act 2018 which are repealed.

c. paragraph 47(3) amends paragraph 5(1) of Schedule 4 to provide that the temporary power in paragraph 1 of Schedule 4 (the power to provide for fees or charges) can only be used for up to two years after IP completion day, instead of exit day. It will expire at that point;

d. paragraph 47(4) makes further provision consequential on the repeal of section 9;

e. paragraph 47(5) amends paragraph 8(a) to explain that an appropriate authority (means a Minister of Crown or devolved authority) is defined as one that could have made a modification under the ECA prior to IP completion day, instead of exit day; and

f. paragraph 47(6) makes further provision consequential on the repeal of section 9;

558 Paragraph 48 amends Schedule 5 (publication and rules of evidence):

a. paragraph 48(1) introduces the amendments to Schedule 5;

b. paragraph 48(2) substitutes 'IP completion day' for all references to 'exit day' in Schedule 5, paragraphs 1(1)(a), 5(a) and (b) and 2(1). This ensures that the Queen's Printer will have various duties and powers conferred upon it, to ensure that retained EU law is made accessible, and published, after IP completion day;

c. paragraph 48(3) amends paragraph 3 of Schedule 5:

   i. paragraph 48(3)(a) amends paragraph 3(1) of Schedule 5, so that to the extent that determining the meaning or effect of EU law is necessary for any legal proceedings (including for the purpose of interpreting retained EU law and the Agreements), judges will determine the meaning or effect themselves as a question of law, rather than treat it is a question of fact; and

   ii. paragraph 48(3)(b) omits the definition of 'interpreting retained EU law' from paragraph 3(2) of Schedule 5 to correspond with the change to paragraph 3(1).

d. paragraph 48(4) amends paragraph 4 of Schedule 5:

   i. paragraph 48(4)(a) amends sub-paragraph (4) to enable regulations providing for evidential rules to modify legislation which is passed or made before IP completion day;

   ii. paragraph 48(4)(b) amends sub-paragraph (5):

      1. paragraph 48(4)(b)(i) inserts the Agreements into definition of a 'relevant matter' in respect of which regulations can be made under this paragraph; and

      2. paragraph 48(4)(b)(ii) makes sure that anything specified in the regulations that relates to the Agreement is also included in the definition of 'relevant matter'.

These Explanatory Notes relate to the European Union (Withdrawal Agreement) Act 2020 (c.1) which received Royal Assent on 23 January 2020

559 Paragraph 49 amends Schedule 6 of the EU (Withdrawal) Act 2018 (Instruments which are exempt EU instruments):

    a.   paragraph 49(1) introduces the amendments to Schedule 6;

    b.   paragraph 49(2) removes paragraphs 1(1), 2 and 4 from inclusion in Schedule 6. These paragraphs set out which EU instruments are 'exempt' under the preservation of direct EU legislation in section 3 of the EU (Withdrawal) Act 2018. These exemptions are no longer necessary. These EU instruments will not be preserved under the amended section 3 which will be limited to EU instruments which are applicable to and in the UK at the end of the implementation period; and

    c.   paragraph 49(3) amends paragraph 3 of Schedule 6, by omitting "or EU regulation" in paragraph 3(b) of Schedule 6 and omitting paragraph 3(b) (which concerns EU directive which is not applicable to the UK immediately before exit day) as these exclusions are no longer needed.

560 Paragraph 50 amends paragraph 2(17) in Part 1 of Schedule 7 of the EU (Withdrawal) Act 2018 to bring into the scope of that paragraph sub-paragraph (16) of paragraph 2 of Schedule 7.

561 Paragraph 51 amends Part 1 of Schedule 7 to insert the scrutiny procedures for powers that will be inserted into the EU (Withdrawal Act) 2018.

Powers in connection with Part 4 of the Withdrawal Agreement

562 New paragraph 8A and 8B sets out the parliamentary scrutiny procedures that will apply to the new powers in the EU (Withdrawal) Act 2018 in connection with Part 4 of the Withdrawal Agreement:

    a.   section 8A establishes that instruments made under new section 1A(3)(a)(ii) of the Act is subject to the draft affirmative procedure (i.e. approved by a resolution of each House of Parliament); and

    b.   section 8B provides that where the new section 8A power modifies primary legislation or retained direct principal legislation, it will be subject to the affirmative procedure. Otherwise, the power will be subject to the negative procedure. The equivalent scrutiny procedures in the devolved legislatures are applicable to the devolved authorities acting alone under the powers in Part 1A of Schedule 2 to the EU (Withdrawal) Act 2018;

563 New paragraph 8C deals with scrutiny by the UK Parliament and the devolved legislatures for instruments made jointly by a Minister of the Crown and a devolved authority.

Powers in connection with other separation issues in the Withdrawal Agreement etc.

564 New paragraph 8D sets out the parliamentary scrutiny procedures that will apply to regulations made by UK Ministers under new section 8B:

    a.   8D(1) establishes that instruments that amend, repeal or revoke primary legislation or retained direct principal EU legislation may not be made unless a draft has been laid before and approved by both Houses; and

    b.   8D(2) sets out that any other instruments made under this power are subject to annulment by either House.

565 New paragraph 8D(3) to (8) sets out the scrutiny procedures that will apply to regulations made by Scottish Ministers, Welsh Ministers or Northern Ireland departments under the power at new Part 1B of Schedule 2; and

These Explanatory Notes relate to the European Union (Withdrawal Agreement) Act 2020 (c.1) which received Royal Assent on 23 January 2020

78

566 New paragraph 8E sets out the scrutiny procedures that will apply to regulations made under new Part 1B of Schedule 2 by a UK Minister acting jointly with a devolved authority.

Powers in connection with Ireland/Northern Protocol in the Withdrawal Agreement

567 New paragraph 8F sets out the parliamentary scrutiny procedures that will apply to regulations made under new section 8C and new Part 1C of Schedule 2:

    a. 8F(1) provides that the affirmative procedure must be used if an instrument made under section 8C(1) does one or more of the things listed at sub-paragraph 8F(2):

        i. amends, repeals or revokes primary legislation or retained direct principal EU legislation;

        ii. establishes a public authority;

        iii. relates to a fee in respect of a function exercisable by a public authority in the UK;

        iv. creates, or widens the scope of, a criminal offence;

        v. creates or amends a power to legislate; or

        vi. facilitates the access to the market within Great Britain of qualifying Northern Ireland goods.

    b. 8F(3) sets out that any other instruments made under this power are subject to the negative procedure (i.e. subject to resolution of either House of the parliament); and

    c. 8F(4) provides that the affirmative procedure must be used where regulations define 'qualifying Northern Ireland goods' under new section 8C(6).

568 New sub-paragraphs 8F(5) to (10) set out the scrutiny procedures that will apply to regulations made by Scottish Ministers, Welsh Ministers or Northern Ireland departments under the power at new Part 1C of Schedule 2.

569 New paragraph 8G sets out the scrutiny procedures by the UK Parliament and the devolved legislatures for instruments made under new Part 1C of Schedule 2 by a Minister of the Crown acting jointly with a devolved authority.

570 Paragraph 52 amends Part 2 of Schedule 7 (scrutiny of other powers under Act) to the European Union (Withdrawal) Act 2018.

571 Paragraph 52(1) introduces the amendment;

572 Paragraph 52(2) inserts a new paragraph 9A (power in relation to interpretation of retained EU law) which provides that regulations made under section 6(5A) are subject to the affirmative procedure powers under the Act).

573 Paragraph 52(3) deletes paragraph 10 of Part 2 of Schedule 7. This is consequential on the repeal of section 9 (the power to implement the withdrawal agreement).

574 Paragraph 52(4) deletes "certain implementation or" in paragraph 17 of Part 2 of Schedule 7.This is consequential on the repeal of section 9 (the power to implement the withdrawal agreement).

575 Paragraph 52(5) amends paragraph 17(1) to remove references to paragraph 10. Paragraph 17(11) is amended to remove the definitions of Commons and Lords sitting days which are no longer necessary after the repeal of section 9.

These Explanatory Notes relate to the European Union (Withdrawal Agreement) Act 2020 (c.1) which received Royal Assent on 23 January 2020

79

576 Paragraph 52(6) removes paragraph 18 (Committee of the National Assembly for Wales to sift certain implementation regulations of Welsh Ministers). This is consequential on the repeal of section 9 (the power to implement the withdrawal agreement).

577 Paragraph 52(7) makes further consequential amendments as a result of the repeal of section 9.

578 Paragraph 53 amends Part 3 of Schedule 7 (general provision about powers under Act) in the following way:

    a.   paragraph 53(1) introduces the amendments to Part 3 of Schedule 7;

    b.   paragraph 53(2) amends paragraph 21 of Schedule 7 of the EU (Withdrawal) Act 2018 so that powers to make regulations in the Act can be used to modify or restate in a clearer or more accessible way anything which continues on or after exit day, to be domestic law by virtue of the saving of EU-derived domestic legislation for the implementation period at new section 1B(2);

    c.   paragraph 53(3) amends paragraph 23 of Schedule 7 of the EU (Withdrawal) Act 2018:

        i.   paragraph 53(3)(a) amends sub-paragraph (1) so that the law preserved by new sections 1A and 1B can also be modified by the power to make consequential provision;

        ii.   paragraph 53(3)(b) amends sub-paragraph (2) to clarify that the consequential power in the Act can also be used to modify anything which continues, on or after exit day, to be domestic law by virtue of the saving of EU-derived domestic legislation for the implementation period at 1B(2), if the changes are consequential on repeal of any provision in the ECA;

        iii.   paragraph 53(3)(c) amends sub-paragraph (3) so that the transitional, transitory and savings power in the Act can do things in connection with the repeal of provisions in the ECA or withdrawal from the EU in a way which is additional, or produces different effects, to the changes made by the new sections 1A and 1B of that Act;

        iv.   paragraph 53(3)(d) amends sub-paragraph (4)(b) to clarify that the consequential power can do things in connection with repeals or withdrawal from the EU which are additional, or produces different effects, to the changes made by new sections 1A and 1B of that Act; and

        v.   paragraph 53(3)(e) amends sub-paragraph (5) to clarify that the transitional, transitory and savings and consequential powers can be used to treat any provisions provided for in sub-paragraphs (3) and (4) as anything which continues to be domestic law by virtue of the saving of EU-derived domestic legislation for the implementation period at 1B(2);

    d.   Paragraph 53(4) inserts a new paragraph 23A 'Anticipatory exercise of powers in relation to section 1B(2) saved law' into Schedule 7 of the EU (Withdrawal) Act 2018. New paragraph 23A clarifies the anticipatory use of delegated powers in this Act in relation to any enactment which continues, on or after exit day, to be domestic law by virtue of the saving of EU-derived domestic legislation for the implementation period at 1B(2). This means that these powers can be exercised before exit day to amend domestic law saved by virtue of 1B(2), so that the regulations come into force on or after exit day;

These Explanatory Notes relate to the European Union (Withdrawal Agreement) Act 2020 (c.1) which received Royal Assent on 23 January 2020

80

e. Paragraph 53(5) amends references to 'exit day' in paragraph 24 of Schedule 7 of the EU (Withdrawal) Act 2018 to 'IP completion day'. This means that the delegated powers in the EU (Withdrawal) Act 2018 can be exercised before IP completion day to modify retained EU law, where the regulations come into force on or after IP completion day; and

f. Paragraph 53(6) inserts a new paragraph 24A 'Anticipatory exercise of powers in relation to the withdrawal agreement' into Schedule 7 of the EU (Withdrawal) Act 2018. New paragraph 24A allows for the anticipatory use of delegated powers in the Act which relate to the Withdrawal Agreement. This means regulations can be made before the Withdrawal Agreement is ratified, where the regulations come into force on or after the day on which the Withdrawal Agreement is ratified.

g. Paragraphs 53(7) to (13) make amendments consequential on the repeal of section 9 of the EU (Withdrawal) Act 2018 in relation to explanatory statements for certain powers and replace references to 'exit day' with 'IP completion day' in paragraphs 28(6)(c) and 29(6)(c) of Part 3 of Schedule 7.

579 Paragraph 54 amends Part 1 of Schedule 8 (general consequential provision):

a. Paragraph 54(1) introduces the amendments to Part 1 of Schedule 8;

b. Paragraphs 54(2) and 54(3) substitute references to 'exit day' in paragraphs 1(1) and 2(1) of Schedule 8 of the EU (Withdrawal) Act 2018 to 'IP completion day'. This ensures that existing ambulatory references (that is, cross-references to EU instruments as they may be amended from time to time in the future) will continue to ambulate until IP completion day. After IP completion day, existing ambulatory references to EU Regulations, decisions or tertiary legislation which form part of retained EU law will generally become references to the retained version of those instruments. Other existing ambulatory references will not generally continue to update after IP completion day. Paragraphs 1(1) and 2(1) of Schedule 8 of the EU (Withdrawal) Act 2018 do not apply where any such reference forms part of or is a reference to relevant separation agreement law.

c. Paragraph 54(4) replaces paragraph 7 of Schedule 8 of the EU (Withdrawal) Act 2018. The new paragraph 7 lifts any implied restriction to act compatibly with EU law on exit day and then IP completion day, so far that EU law restriction does not continue to apply under the Withdrawal Agreement. Any implied EU law restriction which continues by virtue of Part 4 of the Withdrawal Agreement will therefore not be lifted until IP completion day. Further, from IP completion day there is no corresponding restriction in relation to retained EU law, so far as it is not relevant separation agreement law. Any restriction that arises by virtue of other Parts of the Withdrawal Agreement will remain after IP completion day;

d. Paragraph 54(5) amends paragraph 8 of Schedule 8 of the EU (Withdrawal) Act 2018 so that existing powers and powers in Acts passed before the end of the implementation period can be exercised to modify retained EU law before IP completion day if they come into force on or after IP completion day;

e. Paragraph 54(6) amends paragraph 9 of Schedule 8 of the EU (Withdrawal) Act 2018 so that it deals with duties to conduct post-implementation reviews of regulations made after IP completion day. In conducting those reviews, Ministers will not need to have regard to how EU Member States have implemented the UK's former EU obligations;

These Explanatory Notes relate to the European Union (Withdrawal Agreement) Act 2020 (c.1) which received Royal Assent on 23 January 2020

81

f. Paragraph 54(7) amends paragraph 12 of Schedule 8 of the EU (Withdrawal) Act 2018 to allow the anticipatory use of future powers so that they can be exercised before IP completion day to amend retained EU law if they come into force on or after IP completion day;

g. Paragraph 54(8), (9), (10) and (11) amend paragraphs 13, 14, 15 and 16 of Schedule 8 of the EU (Withdrawal) Act 2018 so that the additional requirements applying to certain statutory instruments (including Scottish statutory instruments to an extent) that amend or revoke section 2(2) ECA regulations apply from IP completion day. This is in light of the continuing EU obligations on the UK during the implementation period under Part 4 of the Withdrawal Agreement; and

h. These requirements will not apply where the amendment or revocation is only for the purposes of, or otherwise only within the scope of, the Withdrawal Agreement (other than Part 4 of that agreement), the EEA EFTA Separation Agreement, or the Swiss Citizens' Rights Agreement, as the UK will still be subject to international obligations when making such amendments or revocations.

580 Paragraph 55 amends Part 3 of Schedule 8 on general transitional, transitory or saving provision):

a. Paragraph 55(2) inserts new paragraph 36A into Schedule 8 of the EU (Withdrawal) Act 2018. New sub-paragraphs 36(A)(1) and (2) make clear that anything in force or being done in connection with the ECA as saved by new section 1A(2), EU-derived domestic legislation saved by new section 1B(2), for the purpose of implementing EU obligations or otherwise related to EU law immediately before exit day, continues to be in force or being done on and after exit day;

b. Sub-paragraph 36A(3) makes clear that the above provision in this new paragraph is subject to certain sections of the EU (Withdrawal) Act 2018 and the EU (Withdrawal Agreement) Act, and other relevant enactments. 36A(4) clarifies that references to anything being done, includes anything omitted to be done; and

c. Paragraph 55(3) amends paragraph 37 of Schedule 8 of the EU (Withdrawal) Act 2018 so that it functions as intended, by providing for the continuation of existing acts in relation to retained EU law, but on IP completion day when this law will be retained. It also takes account of other related amendments to this Act.

581 Paragraph 56 amends Part 4 of Schedule 8 on specific transitional, transitory and saving provision:

a. Paragraph 56(2) amends the subheading before paragraph 38 of Part 4 of Schedule 4 to the EU (Withdrawal) Act 2018 so that it reads: 'Retention of saved EU law at the end of implementation period';

b. Paragraph 56(3) inserts a new paragraph 37A to make clear that the automatic repeal of the key implementation period provisions in the EU (Withdrawal) Act 2018 on IP completion day will not prevent the glosses which applied to domestic legislation during the implementation period, under section 1B(3), (4) or (5), from applying to that legislation as saved by section 2 of the EU (Withdrawal) Act 2018;

c. Paragraph 56(4) amends references to 'exit day' to 'IP completion day' in paragraph 38 of Schedule 8 to the EU (Withdrawal) Act 2018. This ensures that rights etc which arise under EU directives and are recognised by courts or tribunals in the UK in cases which have begun before IP completion day but are decided on or after IP completion day are preserved by section 4 and are not excluded by subsection (2) of that section;

These Explanatory Notes relate to the European Union (Withdrawal Agreement) Act 2020 (c.1) which received Royal Assent on 23 January 2020

82

d. Paragraph 56(5) amends references to 'exit day' to 'IP completion day' in paragraph 39 of Schedule 8 to the EU (Withdrawal) Act 2018. This makes further provision about the exceptions to the saving and incorporation of EU law set out in section 5 and Schedule 1. This ensures that the transitional and savings provisions for the exceptions to the preservation of EU law take effect from IP completion day;

e. Paragraph 56(6) amends paragraph 40 of Schedule 8 in the EU (Withdrawal) Act 2018 so that new powers which are added to the Act and are sunsetted are added into the name-checked sections to clarify that although these powers expire, the regulations made under them do not expire;

f. Paragraph 56(7) amends references to 'exit day' to 'IP completion day' in paragraph 41 of Schedule 8 in the EU (Withdrawal) Act 2018 so that the validity of devolved primary legislation receiving Royal Assent before IP completion day or subordinate legislation subject to confirmation or approval that has been made or approved before IP completion day and any other subordinate legislation made before IP completion day is not affected;

g. These amendments also disapply the current EU law limit on devolved competence so that primary and secondary legislation can be made validly before IP completion day in relation to an area that is not specific in any regulations made under the powers inserted by section 12(2), 12(4) or 12(6) or Schedule 3, Part 1 as subject to a limit on competence. This amendment also disapplies - for the exercise of the powers in Schedules 2 and 4 - the provisions in the Devolution Acts that would otherwise prevent the devolved administrations from making secondary legislation that would be incompatible with EU law; and

h. Paragraph 56(8) again amends references to 'exit day' to 'IP completion day' in paragraph 42 of Schedule 8 in the EU (Withdrawal) Act 2018. This amendment is self-explanatory.

582 Paragraph 57 makes consequential amendments to the European Parliamentary Elections etc (Repeal, Revocation, Amendment and Saving Provisions) (United Kingdom and Gibraltar) (EU Exit) Regulations 2018 as a result of the conversion of EU law into 'retained EU law' taking place at the end of the implementation period.

Legislation (Wales) Act 2019

583 Paragraphs 58 to 62 amend the Legislation (Wales) Act 2019 (anaw 4) to insert, substitute and amend entries relating to the Withdrawal Agreement and, in particular, the implementation period.

Part 3: Transitional, transitory and saving provision

584 Paragraph 63 makes technical modifications to the new provisions inserted into the Immigration Act 1971 and the UK Borders Act 2007 in order to ensure that these provisions make reference to the correct provisions within the Agreements before the end of the implementation period; and to reflect the fact that the frontier worker and healthcare categories of relevant person will not exist until the end of the implementation period.

585 Paragraph 64 specifies certain provisions of the devolution statutes as not applying to the making of regulations under section 12, 13 or 14. It makes clear that section 56(2) of the Scotland Act 1998, section 80(8) of the Government of Wales Act 2006 and section 24(1)(b) of the Northern Ireland Act 1998, so far as relating to EU law, do not apply to the making of regulations under certain sections of the EU (Withdrawal) Act 2018.

These Explanatory Notes relate to the European Union (Withdrawal Agreement) Act 2020 (c.1) which received Royal Assent on 23 January 2020

83

586 Paragraph 65 is a saving provision in relation to the repeals in section 36(e) and (f). It saves the amendments made by section 2 of the European Union (Withdrawal) Act 2019 and section 4 of the European Union (Withdrawal) (No. 2) Act 2019 to section 20(4) of the EU (Withdrawal) Act 2018, which provides for regulations to be made amending the definition of exit day.

587 Paragraph 66(1) makes clear that powers inserted into the EU (Withdrawal) Act 2018 by this Act, do not affect the scope of other powers in the Act. Paragraph 66(2) makes clear that the modifications made by the Act to powers to make regulations in the EU (Withdrawal) Act 2018 do not affect the validity of any regulations made under those powers before the coming into force of the modifications. This makes clear that these regulations will not be impliedly revoked due to the power changing. Paragraph 66(3) makes clear that this is subject to transitional, transitory or saving provisions made under the powers in section 41(5) of the Act and section 23(6) of the EU (Withdrawal) Act 2018.

588 Paragraph 67 makes clear that regulations made under paragraph 1(3) or 3(2) of this Schedule before the powers are sunset one year after IP completion day will remain in force after this time, although regulations cannot be made under these powers after that date.

589 Paragraph 68(1) provides that the power to make transitional, transitory or saving provision under section 23(6) of the EU (Withdrawal) Act 2018 includes the power to make such provision as the Minister considers appropriate in connection with the coming into force of any provision of that Act as modified by this Act. Paragraph 68(3) clarifies that this includes modifications to provisions of the EU (Withdrawal) Act 2018 which make amendments to other legislation.

590 Paragraph 68(2) makes clear that this does not limit the power to make transitional, transitory or saving provision under section 41(5) of this Act. It also makes clear that the power under section 25(4) of the EU (Withdrawal) Act 2018 to bring into force provisions of that Act does not apply to modifications made to that Act by this Act.

Commencement

591 Section 42(6) sets out the provisions of the Act that will commence on Royal Assent. Section 42(7) sets out that the remaining provisions will commence on the day or days appointed by regulations.

Equalities

592 During the passage of the EU (Withdrawal) Act 2018 through the House of Commons, the previous Government committed to providing a statement on the impact of EU-exit primary legislation on either the Equality Act 2006 or the Equality Act 2010.

593 With certain exceptions set out below, the European Union (Withdrawal Agreement) Act does not amend, repeal or revoke any provision of the Equality Act 2006, the Equality Act 2010 or any subordinate legislation made under either of those Acts (the equalities legislation).

594 Paragraph 21 of Schedule 2 of the Act amends Part 1 of Schedule 19 of the 2010 Act to add the IMA to the list of public bodies which are subject to the public sector equality duty.

These Explanatory Notes relate to the European Union (Withdrawal Agreement) Act 2020 (c.1) which received Royal Assent on 23 January 2020

84

595 Further, there are some EU-related references in the Equalities Acts which will be glossed by the implementation period provisions in the Act. For example, references to the ECA will be read as references to the modified and saved version of the Act and references to EU measures will be read as references to those EU measures as they have effect by virtue of Part 4 of the Withdrawal Agreement. These glosses enable the provisions of the Acts to operate properly during the implementation period, reflecting the UK's new relationship with EU law during that period.

596 In relation to the policy which is given effect by the Act, the Secretary of State has had due regard to the need to eliminate discrimination, harassment, victimisation and any other conduct that is prohibited by or under the Equality Act 2010.

Related documents

597 The following documents are relevant to the Act and can be read at the stated locations:

- Agreement on the withdrawal of the United Kingdom of Great Britain and Northern Ireland from the European Union and the European Atomic Energy Community

- Agreement on arrangements between Iceland, the Principality of Liechtenstein, the Kingdom of Norway and the United Kingdom of Great Britain and Northern Ireland following the withdrawal of the United Kingdom from the European Union, the EEA Agreement and other agreements applicable between the United Kingdom and the EEA EFTA States by virtue of the United Kingdom's membership of the European Union

- Agreement between the United Kingdom of Great Britain and Northern Ireland and the Swiss Confederation on Citizens' rights following the Withdrawal of the United Kingdom from the European Union and the Free Movement of Persons Agreement Instrument relating to the agreement on the withdrawal of the United Kingdom of Great Britain and Northern Ireland from the European Union and the European Atomic Energy Community

- Political Declaration setting out the framework for the future relationship between the European Union and the United Kingdom

- Joint statement supplementing the Political Declaration setting out the framework for the future relationship between the European Union and the United Kingdom of Great Britain and Northern Ireland

- Legislating for the Withdrawal Agreement between the United Kingdom and the European Union

- The European Union (Withdrawal) Act 2018 (Exit Day) (Amendment) (No. 2) Regulations 2019

- The European Union (Withdrawal) Act 2018 (Exit Day) (Amendment) (No.3) Regulations 2019

These Explanatory Notes relate to the European Union (Withdrawal Agreement) Act 2020 (c.1) which received Royal Assent on 23 January 2020

85

Annex A – Territorial extent and application in the United Kingdom

598 This Act extends and applies to the whole of the UK. In addition, repeals and amendments made by the Act have the same territorial extent and application as the legislation that they are repealing or amending.

These Explanatory Notes relate to the European Union (Withdrawal Agreement) Act 2020 (c.1) which received Royal Assent on 23 January 2020

86

Annex B – Hansard References

599 The following table sets out the dates and Hansard references for each stage of the Act's passage through Parliament.

Stage	Date	Hansard Reference
House of Commons		
First Reading	19 December 2019	(no debate)
Second Reading	20 December 2019	Vol. 669 Col. 146
Committee of the Whole House	07 January 2020	First sitting: Vol. 669 Col. 278
	08 January 2020	Second sitting: Vol. 669 Col. 389
Third Reading	09 January 2020	Vol. 669 Col. 652
House of Lords		
First Reading	09 January 2020	Vol. 801 Col. 440
Second Reading	13 January 2020	Vol. 801 Col. 453
Committee of the Whole House	14 January 2020	First sitting: Vol. 801 Col. 572
	15 January 2020	Second sitting: Vol. 801 Col. 664
	16 January 2020	Third sitting: Vol. 801 Col. 828
Report	20 January 2020	First sitting: Vol. 801 Col. 929
	21 January 2020	Second sitting: Vol. 801 Col. 1014
Third Reading	21 January 2020	Vol. 801 Col.1091
Commons Consideration of Lords Amendments	22 January 2020	Vol. 670 Col. 315
Lords Consideration of Commons Reasons and Amendments	22 January 2020	Vol. 801 Col.1136
Royal Assent	23 January 2020	Vol. 670 Col.481

These Explanatory Notes relate to the European Union (Withdrawal Agreement) Act 2020 (c.1) which received Royal Assent on 23 January 2020

Annex C – Glossary

Term	Definition
Act of Parliament	An Act of Parliament is a law that both Houses of Parliament have passed, and which is enforced in all the areas of the UK where it is applicable.
Affirmative procedure	Under the affirmative procedure, a statutory instrument must be approved by both the House of Commons and the House of Lords to become law (or only by the House of Commons if it was laid before that House only). There are two subcategories of the affirmative procedure in this Act. Under the *draft affirmative* procedure, the statutory instrument cannot be made unless a draft has been laid before and approved by both Houses. Under the *made affirmative* procedure, the statutory instrument can be made and come into force before it is debated, but cannot remain in force unless approved by both Houses within a set time period.
Agreements	This is the collective noun used to refer to the Withdrawal Agreement, the EEA EFTA Separation Agreement, and the Swiss Citizens' Rights Agreement.
Act	A proposal for a new law or an amendment to an existing law that has been presented to Parliament for consideration. Once agreed and made into law, it becomes an Act.
Coming into force/Commencement	The process by which an Act of Parliament, secondary legislation or other legal instrument comes to have legal effect. The law applies from the date on which it comes into force but not any sooner. Also known as commencement.
Court of Justice of the European Union (CJEU)	The CJEU has jurisdiction to rule on the interpretation and application of the treaties. In particular, the Court has jurisdiction to rule on challenges to the validity of EU acts, in infraction proceedings brought by the Commission or member states against member states and on references from national courts concerning the interpretation of EU acts. The Court is made up of two sub-courts: the General Court and the Court of Justice (which is sometimes called the ECJ). See Article 19 TEU

These Explanatory Notes relate to the European Union (Withdrawal Agreement) Act 2020 (c.1) which received Royal Assent on 23 January 2020

88

	and Articles 251 to 281 TFEU.
Decision	A legislative act of the EU which is binding upon those to whom it is addressed. If a decision has no addressees, it binds everyone. See Article 288 TFEU.
Delegated Act	A form of EU instrument which is similar to UK secondary legislation. An EU legislative act, such as a directive or a regulation, can delegate power to the Commission to adopt delegated acts to supplement or amend non-essential elements of the legislative act. See Article 290 TFEU.
Devolution settlements	The constitutional arrangements governing which decision-making responsibilities and legislation-making powers have been devolved and the mechanisms through which these operate.
Devolution statutes (or Acts/legislation)	The principal Acts of Parliament that set out the terms of the devolution settlements. These are the Scotland Act 1998, the Northern Ireland Act 1998, and the Government of Wales Act 2006. 'Devolution legislation' may refer either to the devolution statutes or to the statues together with the secondary legislation made under them.
Devolved administrations	The Scottish Government, the Welsh Government and the Northern Ireland Executive.
Devolved authorities	This is a term used in the Act to refer collectively to the devolved authorities in Scotland, Wales and Northern Ireland. This includes ministers in the Scottish and Welsh Governments or a Northern Ireland Department.
Devolved competence	The areas in which the devolved legislatures are responsible for making laws ('legislative competence') or the devolved administrations are responsible for governing or making secondary legislation ('executive competence').
Devolved institutions	Used to refer collectively to both the devolved administrations and the devolved legislatures.

These Explanatory Notes relate to the European Union (Withdrawal Agreement) Act 2020 (c.1) which received Royal Assent on 23 January 2020

89

Devolved legislatures	The Scottish Parliament, the National Assembly for Wales and the Northern Ireland Assembly.
Directive	A legislative act of the EU which requires member states to achieve a particular result without dictating the means of achieving that result. Directives must be transposed into national law using domestic legislation, in contrast to regulations, which are enforceable as law in their own right. See Article 288 TFEU.
ECA	European Communities Act 1972
EEA EFTA Separation Agreement	An international treaty between the UK and EEA EFTA countries (Norway, Iceland and Liechtenstein) that governs the UK's withdrawal from the EEA following the UK's exit from the EU.
EEA Regulations 2016	Immigration (European Economic Area) Regulations 2016
EU institutions	There are a number of EU bodies which are defined under the Treaties as EU institutions including the European Parliament, the European Council, the Council of the European Union and the European Commission.
The EU Treaties (including TEU and TFEU)	The European Economic Community (EEC) was established by the Treaty of Rome in 1957. This Treaty has since been amended and supplemented by a series of treaties, the latest of which is the Treaty of Lisbon. The Treaty of Lisbon, which entered into force on 1 December 2009, re-organised the two treaties on which the European Union is founded: the Treaty on European Union (TEU) and the Treaty establishing the European Community, which was re-named the Treaty on the Functioning of the European Union (TFEU).
EU (Withdrawal) Act 2018	European Union (Withdrawal) Act 2018.
European Convention on Human Rights (ECHR)	An international convention, ratified by the UK and incorporated into domestic law in the Human Rights Act 1998. It specifies a list of protected Human Rights, and establishes a Court (European Court of Human Rights sitting in Strasbourg) to determine breaches of those rights. All member states are

These Explanatory Notes relate to the European Union (Withdrawal Agreement) Act 2020 (c.1) which received Royal Assent on 23 January 2020

90

	parties to the Convention. The Convention is a Council of Europe Convention, which is a different organisation from the EU. Article 6 TEU provides for the EU to accede to the ECHR.
European Council	The European Council defines the general political direction and priorities of the EU. It consists of the Heads of State or Government of the member states, together with its President and the President of the Commission. See Article 15 TEU and Articles 235 and 236 TFEU.
European Parliament	The European Parliament (EP) consists of representatives elected by Union citizens. The EP shares legislative and budgetary power with the Council, and has oversight over the actions of the Commission. See Article 14 TEU and Articles 223 to 234 TFEU.
Exit day	The day the UK leaves the EU.
FMOPA	EU-Swiss Free Movement of Persons Agreement.
Glosses	Non-textual modifications to legislation (i.e. reading X as Y). For example used to make clear the way that EU law terms should be read on the UK statute book, so that our laws continue to work during the implementation period. This includes ensuring that across the UK statute book, references to 'EU citizens', will be read as including UK nationals for the duration of the implementation period.
IP completion day	The day that the implementation period ends - 31 December 2020 at 11.00 p.m., as provided for in Part 4 of the Withdrawal Agreement
IMA	The Independent Monitoring Authority for the Citizens' Rights Agreements.
Joint Committees	Joint Committees established by Article 164 of the Withdrawal Agreement, Article 65 of the EEA EFTA Separation Agreement, Article 6 of the Swiss Citizens' Rights Agreement.
Negative procedure	A statutory instrument under the negative procedure becomes law once it is made and laid before Parliament, but will normally

These Explanatory Notes relate to the European Union (Withdrawal Agreement) Act 2020 (c.1) which received Royal Assent on 23 January 2020

91

not come into force until at least 21 calendar days after it has been made. Under the negative procedure, an instrument may be annulled by resolution of either House of Parliament (or only by the House of Commons if it was laid before that House only) within a period of 40 calendar days of it having been laid, not including any period when both Houses (or just the House of Commons) are adjourned for more than four days.

Regulation	A legislative act of the EU which is directly applicable in member states without the need for national implementing legislation (as opposed to a directive, which must be transposed into domestic law by member states using domestic legislation). See Article 288 TFEU.
Secondary legislation	Legal instruments (including regulations and orders) made under powers delegated to ministers or other office holders in Acts of Parliament. They have the force of law but can be disapplied by a court if they do not comply with the terms of their parent Act. Also called subordinate or delegated legislation.
Statute book	The body of legislation that has been enacted by Parliament or one of the devolved legislatures and has effect in the UK.
Statutory instrument	A form of secondary legislation to which the Statutory Instruments Act 1946 applies.
Swiss Citizens' Rights Agreement	An international treaty between the UK and Switzerland that protects the rights of Swiss nationals in the UK and UK nationals in Switzerland.
Withdrawal Agreement	The 'agreement on the withdrawal of the United Kingdom of Great Britain and Northern Ireland from the European Union and the European Atomic Energy Community'. An international treaty between the UK and the EU that governs the terms of the UK's exit from the EU.

These Explanatory Notes relate to the European Union (Withdrawal Agreement) Act 2020 (c.1) which received Royal Assent on 23 January 2020